Better Homes and Gardens®

LOW-SALT
Cooking

© 1983 by Meredith Corporation, Des Moines, Iowa.
All Rights Reserved. Printed in the United States of America.
First Edition. First Printing.
Library of Congress Catalog Card Number: 83-61318
ISBN: 0-696-01320-7

BETTER HOMES AND GARDENS® BOOKS

Editor: Gerald M. Knox
Art Director: Ernest Shelton
Managing Editor: David A. Kirchner

Food and Nutrition Editor: Nancy Byal
Department Head, Cook Books: Sharyl Heiken
Associate Department Heads: Sandra Granseth,
  Rosemary C. Hutchinson, Elizabeth Woolever
Senior Food Editors: Julie Henderson, Julia Malloy, Marcia Stanley
Associate Food Editors: Jill Burmeister, Molly Culbertson,
  Linda Foley, Linda Henry, Joyce Trollope, Diane Yanney
Recipe Development Editor: Marion Viall
Test Kitchen Director: Sharon Stilwell
Test Kitchen Home Economists: Jean Brekke, Kay Cargill, Marilyn Cornelius,
  Maryellyn Krantz, Dianna Nolin, Marge Steenson

Associate Art Directors: Linda Ford Vermie, Neoma Alt West, Randall Yontz
Copy and Production Editors: Marsha Jahns, Mary Helen Schiltz,
  Carl Voss, David A. Walsh
Assistant Art Directors: Harijs Priekulis, Tom Wegner
Senior Graphic Designers: Alisann Dixon, Lynda Haupert, Lyne Neymeyer
Graphic Designers: Mike Burns, Mike Eagleton, Deb Miner,
  Stan Sams, D. Greg Thompson, Darla Whipple, Paul Zimmerman

Vice President, Editorial Director: Doris Eby
Group Editorial Services Director: Duane L. Gregg

General Manager: Fred Stines
Director of Publishing: Robert B. Nelson
Vice President, Retail Marketing: Jamie Martin
Vice President, Direct Marketing: Arthur Heydendael

LOW-SALT COOKING
Editor: Jill Burmeister
Copy and Production Editor: David A. Walsh
Graphic Designer: Alisann Dixon
Electronic Text Processor: Joyce Wasson

 Our seal assures you that every recipe in *Low-Salt Cooking* has been tested in the Better Homes and Gardens® Test Kitchen. This means that each recipe is practical and reliable, and meets our high standards of taste appeal.

On the front cover:
Orange-Vegetable Beef Roast (see recipe variation, page 27)

Contents

LOW-SALT COOKING
A LIFE-STYLE

In search of flavor

The salt shaker is a common centerpiece on American tables. If at first bite our taste buds don't tingle with a salty sensation, we automatically reach for the salt shaker. In doing so, we overpower—instead of enhance—the true flavors of our food.

Most of us consume much more salt than we really need. If you're one of the growing number of people who want to cut back on salt, let *Low-Salt Cooking* help you. To be honest, you're bound to notice a difference when you use less salt. However, the bold, well-rounded flavors of these recipes minimize that difference. After you become accustomed to low-salt eating, you'll find that many of the foods you previously thought tasted just right seem too salty. You'll discover taste sensations you've been missing all along and learn to appreciate food flavors for what they really are.

Shake the habit at the table

The first step to lowering salt intake is to leave the salt shaker off the table. Instead, use the pepper shaker or, better yet, freshly ground pepper. Keep lemon wedges handy for squeezing over vegetables, poultry, and fish. Place a cruet of vinegar on the table to perk up salads and meats. (To make your own herb vinegar, see the tip on page 13.) If you feel you must add salt, use one shake instead of two.

Alter your cooking habits

To allow your taste buds to adjust to lower salt levels, cut back gradually on the amount of salt you use when you cook. By seasoning with herbs, spices, vinegar, wine, citrus fruits, onions, and garlic, you can reduce or eliminate added salt without losing flavor. When cooking rice, noodles, or pasta, leave out the salt; the food you usually serve with it provides ample flavor.

Whenever possible, cook from scratch. When you choose each ingredient, you control the amount of salt in the food. Use fresh or unprocessed ingredients instead of processed foods, which usually contain more salt.

Sneaky sodium

Sodium, a major component of salt, is prevalent in the foods we eat each day. It's probably no surprise to anyone that potato chips are high in sodium; you can see and taste the salt. But did you know that peanut butter and most canned soups also are loaded? Get to know which foods are high in sodium so you can limit their use.

Sausages, luncheon meats, frankfurters, ham, and bacon contain large amounts of salt. So do canned meats such as tuna and chicken. Most natural cheeses contain added salt and process cheeses have even more. Salt is an ingredient in regular butter and margarine, too.

Canned vegetables typically are much higher in salt than their frozen counterparts, which are only slightly higher than the fresh versions. Expect higher sodium counts for vegetables that are canned or frozen with a sauce.

Avoid snack items with added salt such as salted peanuts, pretzels, popcorn, and corn chips. Baked goods such as breads, crackers, cakes, and cookies contain a surprising amount of sodium from added salt, baking soda, or baking powder. Most ready-to-eat cereals or instant hot cereals also have a significant sodium content.

Often, the condiments we add as final touches to foods add as much or more sodium than the foods themselves. Catsup, chili sauce, tartar sauce, Worcestershire sauce, mustard, soy sauce, and mayonnaise are but a few of the popular sodium-laden refinements. Relish-tray favorites such as pickles and olives are extremely salty.

If you don't like the idea of cutting out your favorite high-sodium foods, try a low-sodium version if available. Or, use the recipes in this book to make your own low-sodium staples. The chart on the following page will convince you that the sodium savings is significant.

See the chart starting on page 88 for a complete list of common foods and their sodium content.

Read the label

To become sodium-wise about the foods you eat, get in the habit of reading food labels. More and more manufacturers are voluntarily putting sodium information on their labels. Even when specific sodium amounts are not given, you can look at the ingredients to see whether salt (or salty ingredients) is included. The closer to the beginning it appears in the ingredient list, the more predominant it is in the product.

SODIUM COMPARISON CHART

The ingredients listed in recipes throughout this book are standard commercial products, unless stated otherwise. To cut the sodium in a recipe even further, use low-sodium products or try making your own using recipes in the book. Use the chart below to compare the sodium content of the standard commercial, low-sodium commercial, and low-sodium homemade versions.

	standard commercial product	low-sodium commercial product	low-sodium homemade recipe*
¼ cup barbecue sauce	510 mg	—	21mg
1 biscuit	272 mg	1 mg	18 mg
1 tablespoon butter	140 mg	2 mg	14 mg
1 tablespoon catsup	156 mg	3 mg	3 mg
1 cup chicken broth	722 mg	55 mg	26 mg
1 teaspoon Dijon-style mustard	65 mg	—	1 mg
¼ cup granola	61 mg	16 mg	5 mg
1 tablespoon mayonnaise	84 mg	—	1 mg
1 tablespoon peanut butter	97 mg	1 mg	1 mg
1 teaspoon soy sauce	440 mg	180 mg	120 mg
1 cup tomatoes (canned)	390 mg	16 mg	—
1 cup tomato sauce	1,521 mg	50 mg	48 mg

*See index for page numbers

NUTRITION ANALYSIS

At the beginning of each chapter you will find a nutrition analysis chart giving you the amount of sodium, calories, protein, carbohydrate, fat, and potassium in each serving of a recipe. The chart also gives the percentages of the United States Recommended Daily Allowances (U.S. RDAs) for protein and certain vitamins and minerals per serving. This information was obtained by computerized method using Agriculture Handbook Number 456 as the primary source. Home and Garden Bulletin Number 233 was used as a secondary source. Both are published by the United States Department of Agriculture.

In compiling the nutrition analyses, we made the following assumptions:

• Recipe ingredients used are standard commercial products unless otherwise specified.
• Garnishes and optional ingredients were not included in nutrition analyses.
• If a food was marinated and then brushed with marinade during cooking, the analysis includes the entire marinade amount.
• When two ingredient options appear in a recipe, calculations were made using the first choice.
• For ingredients of variable weight (such as "2½- to 3-pound broiler-fryer chicken"), calculations were made using the lesser weight.
• If a recipe gives a range of servings (such as "Makes 4 to 6 servings"), calculations were made using the smaller number.

Homemade Ingredients

Many items we often use to season
and sauce our foods are surprisingly high in sodium.
By making your own ingredients and condiments,
you can be sure the sodium is low and the quality is high.

HOMEMADE INGREDIENTS	SODIUM (mg)	Calories	Protein (g)	Carbohydrate (g)	Fat (g)	Potassium (mg)	Protein	Vitamin A	Vitamin C	Thiamine	Riboflavin	Niacin	Calcium	Iron
	Per serving						Percent U.S. RDA Per Serving							
Lemon Fines Herbes (p. 14)	0	0	0	0	0	0	0	0	0	0	0	0	0	0
Low-Sodium Barbecue Sauce (p. 12)	16	56	1	5	4	129	1	9	11	2	1	2	1	3
Low-Sodium Blender Peanut Butter (p. 8)	1	83	3	3	7	92	5	0	0	3	1	11	1	2
Low-Sodium Catsup (p. 11)	3	10	0	2	0	63	0	4	5	1	1	1	0	1
Low-Sodium Chicken Broth (p. 14)	26	26	1	6	0	170	2	42	14	2	2	1	2	2
Low-Sodium Dijon-Style Mustard (p. 11)	1	8	0	1	0	9	0	0	0	0	0	0	0	0
Low-Sodium Mayonnaise (p. 9)	1	105	0	0	12	2	0	1	1	0	0	0	0	0
Low-Sodium Peanut-Butter (p. 8)	1	76	3	3	6	92	5	0	0	3	1	11	1	2
Low-Sodium Refrigerator Pickles (p. 10)	2	50	0	13	0	52	0	1	6	1	1	0	1	2
Low-Sodium Soy Sauce (p. 14)	120	1	0	0	0	3	0	0	0	0	0	0	0	0
Low-Sodium Taco Sauce (p. 12)	1	10	0	1	0	60	0	4	9	1	1	1	0	1
Low-Sodium Tomato Sauce (p. 12)	12	79	2	8	5	378	3	25	56	6	4	5	2	4
Sweet Butter (p. 9)	14	41	1	1	4	39	1	3	1	1	3	0	3	0

LOW-SODIUM PEANUT BUTTER

*Cocktail peanuts usually give a smoother texture
than dry roasted peanuts.*

2 cups unsalted cocktail *or* unsalted dry roasted peanuts

Place the steel blade in the work bowl of a food processor; add peanuts. Cover and process till a butter forms, stopping to scrape down sides of bowl occasionally to make sure mixture is evenly blended. Continue processing till butter is desired smoothness. Store in a tightly covered container in the refrigerator. Makes about 1⅓ cups or 22 (1-tablespoon) servings.
• **Low-Sodium Blender Peanut Butter** • Place 1 cup *unsalted cocktail or unsalted dry roasted peanuts* in a blender container. Cover and blend till finely chopped. Gradually blend in 2 to 3 teaspoons *cooking oil* till of desired consistency. Store in a tightly covered container in the refrigerator. Makes about ⅔ cup or 11 (1-tablespoon) servings.

SWEET BUTTER

You can make sweet butter, also known as unsalted butter, at home by beating whipping cream till it separates. It's easiest to make in a food processor, but an electric mixer will do the job as well. Pictured on page 7.

2 cups whipping cream, well
  chilled
¼ cup crushed ice
  Ice water

Place steel blade in work bowl of a food processor; add cream. Cover and process till the soft mass of whipped cream separates into solids and liquid (2 to 3 minutes). Pour off liquid.

While processor is running, add ice. Be sure to cover feed tube. Process till butter forms a mass on top of the blade.

Pour into a fine sieve to drain. Put the butter in a bowl and press to extract any traces of milk (it will sour if not removed).

Wash the butter by adding ice water and kneading the butter; pour off liquid. Repeat till liquid stays clear. Press out all liquid. Pack butter into a crock; cover and refrigerate 48 hours to develop flavor before serving. Makes 1 cup or 16 (1-tablespoon) servings.

• Shaping Butter • For curls, dip a wooden or metal curler into hot water, then pull it across slightly softened butter, guiding the butter into a curl as you pull. Chill the curls in ice water.

For molded butter, dip mold in boiling water, then in ice water. Fill with softened butter, pressing firmly; chill. Remove butter from mold using plunger or by pressing or tapping, depending on the type of mold.

For butter balls, dip a melon ball cutter in hot water, then scoop out cold butter; chill. Or use butter paddles. Cut the butter into equal-sized pieces and let stand at room temperature till slightly softened. Moisten the paddles first in boiling water and then in ice water. Using one piece of butter at a time, roll it between the paddles while moving the paddles in opposite directions in tight circles. Chill balls in ice water.

LOW-SODIUM MAYONNAISE

½ teaspoon dry mustard
¼ teaspoon paprika
  Several dashes ground red
  pepper
2 egg yolks
2 tablespoons vinegar
2 cups salad oil
2 tablespoons lemon juice

In a small mixer bowl combine mustard, paprika, and red pepper. Add egg yolks and vinegar; beat with an electric mixer on medium speed till blended. Add ¼ *cup* of the salad oil, 1 teaspoon at a time, beating constantly.

While continuing to beat, add remaining oil in a thin, steady stream, alternating the last ½ cup oil with the lemon juice. Store in a tightly covered jar in the refrigerator for up to 1 month. Makes about 2⅓ cups or 38 (1-tablespoon) servings.

LOW-SODIUM REFRIGERATOR PICKLES

*Tucked into a sandwich or alone on a relish tray, these pickles will please
even the salt-lover's palate.*

6	**cups thinly sliced cucumbers**
2	**cups thinly sliced onions**
1	**clove garlic, halved**
1½	**cups sugar**
1½	**cups vinegar**
½	**teaspoon mustard seed**
½	**teaspoon celery seed**
½	**teaspoon ground turmeric**

In a glass or crockery bowl place thinly sliced cucumbers, onions, and garlic. In a saucepan combine sugar, vinegar, mustard seed, celery seed, and turmeric; bring to boiling, stirring just till the sugar is dissolved. Pour vinegar mixture over the cucumber mixture. Cover and chill at least 24 hours before serving. Store in the refrigerator for up to 1 month. Makes 7 cups or 28 (¼-cup) servings.

Low-Sodium Refrigerator Pickles

LOW-SODIUM CATSUP

Pictured on page 7.

4 cups water
3 6-ounce cans tomato paste
¾ cup chopped onion
½ cup cider vinegar
⅓ cup sugar
1 tablespoon molasses
2 teaspoons dry mustard
½ teaspoon celery seed
¼ teaspoon ground cinnamon
¼ teaspoon ground cloves
¼ teaspoon dried basil, crushed
¼ teaspoon dried tarragon, crushed
¼ teaspoon pepper
1 clove garlic, minced

In a blender container or food processor bowl combine *1 cup* water, *1 can* tomato paste, the onion, vinegar, sugar, molasses, dry mustard, celery seed, cinnamon, cloves, basil, tarragon, pepper, and garlic. Cover and blend or process till smooth.

Pour mixture into a Dutch oven. Stir in the remaining 3 cups water and 2 cans tomato paste. Bring to boiling; reduce heat. Simmer, uncovered, about 35 minutes or till mixture is reduced to half its original volume, stirring occasionally. Pour into jars and store in refrigerator for up to 1 month. (*Or,* follow directions below for water-bath canning or for freezing.) Makes about 5 cups or 80 (1-tablespoon) servings.
• **Water-Bath Canning** • Pour hot catsup into hot, clean half-pint jars, leaving a ¼-inch headspace. Wipe jar rims; adjust lids. Process in a boiling water bath for 10 minutes (start timing when water boils).
• **Freezing** • Cool catsup slightly. Pour into moisture-vapor-proof freezer containers, leaving a ½-inch headspace. Cool completely. Seal, label, and freeze for up to 10 months.

LOW-SODIUM DIJON-STYLE MUSTARD

Make a double batch so you'll have enough for gifts. To double the recipe, double the ingredients and add 5 minutes to each cooking step. Pictured on page 7.

1 cup dry white wine
½ cup vinegar
¼ cup chopped onion
1 tablespoon sugar
½ teaspoon dried tarragon, crushed
5 whole allspice
2 cloves garlic, minced
1 bay leaf
   Dash ground red pepper
½ cup dry mustard
¼ cup cold water

In a 1-quart saucepan combine wine, vinegar, onion, sugar, tarragon, allspice, garlic, bay leaf, and red pepper. Bring mixture to boiling. Boil, uncovered, over medium-high heat about 20 minutes or till liquid is reduced by half. Meanwhile, in a bowl stir together dry mustard and cold water; let stand at least 10 minutes.

Strain vinegar mixture into mustard mixture, pressing out all liquid; discard solids. Stir vinegar-mustard mixture; return to the saucepan. Cook, uncovered, over medium-low heat about 10 minutes or to the consistency of heavy cream, stirring frequently. (Mixture will thicken slightly as it cools.) Cool; cover and refrigerate. Store in refrigerator for up to 2 months. Makes about ¾ cup or 36 (1-teaspoon) servings.

Homemade Ingredients

LOW-SODIUM TOMATO SAUCE

½ cup chopped onion
¼ cup chopped celery
1 clove garlic, minced
2 tablespoons cooking oil *or* olive oil
2 pounds ripe tomatoes, cut up (6 or 7 medium tomatoes)
½ teaspoon sugar

In a large saucepan cook onion, celery, and garlic in oil till vegetables are tender but not brown. Stir in tomatoes, sugar, and ¼ teaspoon *pepper*. Bring to boiling; reduce heat. Boil gently, uncovered, about 40 minutes or to desired consistency, stirring occasionally. Pass through food mill or sieve. Discard skins and seeds. Use in a recipe as tomato sauce or heat and serve over hot cooked pasta. Store in the refrigerator. Makes 1½ cups or 6 (¼-cup) servings.

LOW-SODIUM BARBECUE SAUCE
---

1 6-ounce can tomato paste
½ cup chopped onion
½ cup red wine vinegar
¼ cup cooking oil
2 tablespoons sugar
2 teaspoons celery seed
2 teaspoons paprika
2 teaspoons Worcestershire sauce
1 teaspoon dried oregano, crushed
½ teaspoon chili powder
⅛ teaspoon ground cloves
2 bay leaves
2 cloves garlic, minced

In a 2-quart saucepan combine the tomato paste, onion, vinegar, oil, sugar, celery seed, paprika, Worcestershire sauce, oregano, chili powder, cloves, bay leaves, garlic, and 1½ cups *water*. Bring to boiling; reduce heat. Simmer, uncovered, about 30 minutes or to desired consistency, stirring occasionally. Discard bay leaves. Store in a covered container in refrigerator for up to 2 weeks. (*Or,* pour into 1- or 2-cup freezer containers; seal, label, and freeze. To use, thaw sauce.) Use to baste chicken, beef, or pork the last 10 to 15 minutes of barbecuing. Makes about 2⅔ cups sauce or 14 (3-tablespoon) servings.

LOW-SODIUM TACO SAUCE

This is a fairly mild sauce so if you like it hotter, add more crushed red pepper.
Pictured on page 24.

1½ pounds ripe tomatoes, peeled and quartered (4 medium)
1 medium onion, cut up
1 clove garlic, minced
1 tablespoon cooking oil
1 teaspoon crushed red pepper
1 teaspoon vinegar
½ teaspoon sugar

Place tomatoes in a blender container. Cover and blend till nearly smooth. Measure 2 cups; return to blender container. (Save any remaining for another use.) Add onion, garlic, oil, red pepper, vinegar, and sugar. Cover and blend till smooth. Pour into a 1½-quart saucepan. Bring to boiling; reduce heat. Cook, uncovered, over medium-low heat about 10 minutes or to desired consistency, stirring occasionally. Store in refrigerator. Makes 2 cups sauce or 32 (1-tablespoon) servings.

Making Fresh-Herb Vinegars

Vinegars flavored with fresh herbs do double duty to liven up low-salt foods. The vinegar tang tricks the taste buds so you don't miss the salt, and the subtle herb adds flavor.

To make herb vinegar, start with a cider, white, or white wine vinegar. Add your choice of fresh herb, such as tarragon, thyme, dill, chives, oregano, sage, or basil. Use 1 cup loosely packed leaves per 2 cups vinegar. If you like, add a garlic clove or a twist of lemon peel. Let stand a few days, then strain. The longer the herb is in the vinegar, the stronger the flavor. Pour into a sterilized bottle and seal.

Fresh-Herb Vinegars

Homemade Ingredients

LEMON FINES HERBES

Fines herbes is an herb blend used to season soups, stews, egg dishes, and meats. This lemon version adds a remarkably fresh flavor to low-salt dishes. Start with ¼ teaspoon for 4 servings and add more to suit your taste. Pictured on page 7.

2 large lemons
1 tablespoon dried thyme
1 tablespoon dried savory
1 tablespoon dried marjoram
1 tablespoon dried leaf sage, crushed
1 tablespoon dried basil

Finely shred the yellow peel from the lemons. (Save remainder of lemons for another use.) Spread peel in a shallow baking pan. Dry in a 300° oven about 10 minutes, stirring occasionally. Combine thyme, savory, marjoram, sage, basil, and dried lemon peel. Mix together thoroughly. Store in an airtight container. Crush seasoning before using. Makes ⅓ cup.

LOW-SODIUM CHICKEN BROTH

The artful use of seasoning and the concentration of flavors during cooking make this an outstanding, full-bodied broth.

Bony chicken pieces
(backs, necks, and wings) from
2 chickens
1 stalk celery with leaves, cut up
1 carrot, cut up
1 large onion with skin, quartered
4 sprigs parsley
3 whole cloves
1 bay leaf
½ teaspoon dried thyme, crushed
¼ teaspoon pepper

In a large stockpot or Dutch oven place chicken pieces, celery, carrot, onion, parsley, cloves, bay leaf, thyme, and pepper. Add 6 cups *cold water.* Bring to boiling; reduce heat. Cover and simmer for 1 hour. Uncover; boil gently about 1 hour more. Remove large pieces. Strain broth by ladling it through a sieve lined with 1 or 2 layers of cheesecloth. Discard solids. If using the broth while hot, skim fat. (*Or,* chill broth and lift off fat.)

Store broth in the refrigerator for several days or in the freezer for up to 6 months. Makes 4 (1-cup) servings.

LOW-SODIUM SOY SAUCE

¾ cup water
2 tablespoons instant beef bouillon granules
2 teaspoons red wine vinegar
1 teaspoon molasses
⅛ teaspoon ground ginger
Several dashes pepper
Dash garlic powder

In a small saucepan combine water, beef bouillon granules, red wine vinegar, molasses, ginger, pepper, and garlic powder. Boil gently, uncovered, about 5 minutes or till mixture is reduced to ½ cup. Store in the refrigerator. Stir before using. Makes ½ cup or 24 (1-teaspoon) servings.

Pictured opposite: Orange-Vegetable Pork Roast

Main Dishes

MAIN DISHES	SODIUM (mg)	Calories	Protein (g)	Carbohydrate (g)	Fat (g)	Potassium (mg)	Protein	Vitamin A	Vitamin C	Thiamine	Riboflavin	Niacin	Calcium	Iron
	Per Serving						Percent U.S. RDA Per Serving							
BEEF														
Austrian Caraway Steak Strips (p. 22)	119	539	29	30	31	626	44	48	10	18	22	35	9	26
Brisket Carbonnade (p. 20)	99	350	27	8	21	497	42	1	6	10	16	34	3	24
Country Meat Loaf with Apple Butter Sauce (p. 26)	80	283	21	25	11	464	33	5	10	9	13	23	3	21
Dilled Beef Stroganoff (p. 23)	99	396	22	36	15	593	35	4	6	19	26	35	9	23
Individual Beef Wellingtons (p. 18)	123	900	28	42	68	541	43	21	5	31	32	44	5	29
Italian Eggplant Beef Stew (p. 20)	89	435	24	17	27	948	38	22	81	16	20	36	5	27
London Broil (p. 19)	69	228	20	0	16	314	30	0	0	6	10	24	1	16
Orange-Vegetable Beef Roast (p. 27)	154	605	43	28	35	1095	65	95	121	21	29	53	7	40
Oriental Beef Stir-Fry (p. 23)	83	243	17	12	14	532	26	60	67	9	17	23	6	17
Roast Beef au Poivre (p. 19)	85	434	24	1	34	409	37	1	1	7	13	29	2	20
Savory Steak and Vegetables (p. 22)	171	363	26	18	21	1141	40	190	124	18	24	41	6	32
Spaghetti with Meat Sauce (p. 26)	67	523	23	59	20	982	36	45	105	47	26	43	6	31
Sweet and Sour Chili (p. 25)	83	267	22	25	10	781	34	28	70	15	16	33	3	26
Taco-Style Spuds (p. 25)	138	383	23	37	16	1238	35	38	79	20	19	36	11	24
PORK														
Barbecue-Style Pork Sandwiches (p. 27)	70	359	18	8	28	480	28	10	20	60	14	25	2	19
Brunch Sandwiches (p. 31)	263	515	20	52	26	341	30	7	3	53	20	22	6	22
Creole-Style Lentil Stew (p. 30)	73	394	19	53	13	956	30	35	64	46	19	26	10	29
Curried Pork Chop Platter (p. 31)	92	603	26	46	34	679	41	10	71	87	21	37	4	32
Molasses-Sauced Ribs (p. 33)	91	575	21	21	45	792	33	23	28	70	17	31	6	28
Orange-Vegetable Pork Roast (p. 27)	133	767	36	28	56	997	56	94	121	117	31	49	6	34
Peach-Glazed Pork Roast (p. 28)	100	590	28	21	44	471	43	1	2	90	19	36	2	24
Pork in Cider Sauce (p. 30)	74	542	23	37	33	484	35	5	10	72	19	31	4	25
Skillet Pizza for Two (p. 33)	204	629	29	68	27	757	45	23	65	74	42	45	25	32
Stuffed Cabbage Rolls (p. 32)	132	351	17	13	25	404	26	10	24	48	17	20	9	15
Sweet and Sour Pork (p. 28)	67	510	16	49	27	590	24	32	58	57	16	22	6	19
LAMB														
Lemon-Herb Lamb Chops (p. 36)	73	492	20	3	44	389	31	3	20	13	15	29	2	10
Pocket Lamb Burgers (p. 36)	64	237	17	12	13	448	26	12	25	15	16	22	7	14
POULTRY														
Chicken and Vegetables in Orange Sauce (p. 44)	104	586	44	54	21	1150	67	90	152	34	26	89	8	24
Chicken Breasts à l'Orange (p. 38)	69	360	34	39	7	650	52	8	68	17	17	71	4	12
Chicken in Herbed Yogurt Sauce (p. 41)	100	265	38	6	8	564	59	4	2	6	22	74	7	9
Chicken Piccata (p. 40)	115	331	37	8	13	562	57	9	12	7	19	75	3	11
Chicken Salad Appetizer Puffs (p. 43)	21	68	4	3	5	61	5	1	1	2	2	7	1	1

MAIN DISHES

	SODIUM (mg)	Calories	Protein (g)	Carbohydrate (g)	Fat (g)	Potassium (mg)	Protein	Vitamin A	Vitamin C	Thiamine	Riboflavin	Niacin	Calcium	Iron
	Per Serving						Percent U.S. RDA Per Serving							
POULTRY (continued)														
Chicken Salad in Beer Puffs (p. 43)	91	300	16	13	20	270	24	5	3	8	9	30	3	6
Hawaiian Chicken Rolls (p. 41)	84	394	41	21	16	679	63	8	10	10	24	79	5	17
Lime and Honey Chicken (p. 37)	56	208	20	4	12	247	31	2	7	3	10	37	1	8
Pasta with Chicken, Zucchini, and Tomatoes (p. 43)	120	545	36	58	19	1146	56	45	94	47	37	71	19	21
Seasoned Fried Chicken (p. 38)	55	169	20	3	8	233	31	2	0	5	10	38	1	9
Sesame Chicken (p. 40)	193	298	38	7	12	550	58	1	0	5	17	75	2	9
Sherry-Basted Chicken with Oriental Stuffing (p. 37)	144	528	37	29	27	608	57	29	10	16	20	57	3	21
Turkey Curry (p. 45)	101	360	28	41	9	532	44	3	5	15	16	46	12	12
Waldorf Turkey Toss with Apple Dressing (p. 45)	64	602	27	39	40	580	42	11	9	8	10	41	3	17
FISH														
Broiled Fish with Tropical Tartar Sauce (p. 49)	160	338	37	14	15	696	57	12	36	13	13	20	11	10
Creole Shrimp and Chicken (p. 49)	144	332	30	40	6	968	47	46	130	22	11	46	10	22
Fish Newburg in Chive Crepes (p. 47)	151	341	18	21	20	353	28	20	6	14	21	12	14	9
Skewered Fish and Vegetables (p. 48)	113	257	15	15	16	767	22	36	95	11	9	18	6	10
Tarragon-Mustard Halibut Steaks (p. 47)	159	220	24	2	11	573	36	12	1	4	9	42	2	6
Western-Style Baked Fish (p. 48)	111	196	25	4	8	482	39	12	33	8	7	15	4	7
MEATLESS														
California Omelet (p. 52)	210	286	14	7	23	547	22	40	62	13	30	12	6	17
Hearty Vegetable Stew (p. 50)	357	223	11	32	7	728	16	28	95	13	10	10	6	25
Vegetable Lasagna (p. 52)	345	267	19	35	6	661	29	109	51	26	26	17	13	17
Zucchini-Rice Pie (p. 50)	198	261	12	20	15	301	18	21	15	11	19	9	13	11

Main Dishes

BEEF

INDIVIDUAL BEEF WELLINGTONS

*To cut down on last-minute preparation, assemble the pastry-wrapped fillets
ahead of time and chill. All that's left to do before placing this elegant
entrée before your guests is the baking.*

1 tablespoon cooking oil
¾ teaspoon dried basil, crushed
¼ teaspoon garlic powder
¼ teaspoon pepper
1 pound beef tenderloin, cut into
    four ¾- to 1-inch-thick slices
1½ cups all-purpose flour
3 tablespoons sesame seed,
    toasted
¼ cup unsalted butter *or*
    margarine
¼ cup shortening
1 beaten egg yolk
3 tablespoons cold water
½ teaspoon vinegar
1 cup finely chopped fresh
    mushrooms (4 ounces)
¼ cup sliced green onion
1 tablespoon unsalted butter *or*
    margarine
2 tablespoons burgundy
¼ teaspoon pepper
1 beaten egg yolk
1 tablespoon water

In a small mixing bowl combine cooking oil, basil, garlic powder, and ¼ teaspoon pepper. Rub the tenderloin slices with the herb-oil mixture. Place meat on the rack of an unheated broiler pan. Broil 3 inches from heat, turning once. Allow about 5 minutes total time for rare, about 8 minutes total for medium-rare, or about 10 minutes total for medium. Transfer meat to a plate lined with a double thickness of paper toweling; cover and chill.

Meanwhile, for pastry, combine flour and toasted sesame seed. Cut in ¼ cup unsalted butter or margarine and the shortening till pieces are the size of small peas. Combine 1 beaten egg yolk, 3 tablespoons cold water, and vinegar. Add to flour mixture 1 tablespoon at a time, tossing with a fork till all is moistened. Form into a ball; cover and chill.

In an 8-inch skillet cook mushrooms and green onion in 1 tablespoon unsalted butter or margarine over medium-high heat about 4 minutes or till tender. Stir in burgundy and ¼ teaspoon pepper. Cook 1 to 2 minutes more or till liquid is evaporated. Remove from heat.

Divide pastry into 4 equal parts. On a floured surface roll each into a 7-inch circle. Spoon ¼ of the mushroom mixture in the center of each circle. Place a tenderloin slice atop the mushroom mixture on each circle. Draw pastry up around the meat, trimming off excess dough.

Combine 1 beaten egg yolk and 1 tablespoon water; brush on edges of pastry. Seal edges. Place seam side down on a greased baking sheet. Reroll pastry trimmings; make cutouts. Moisten cutouts with egg yolk mixture and place on pastry-covered meat. (At this point, pastry-covered meat may be covered and chilled till baking time.) Brush remaining egg yolk mixture on top and sides of pastry. Bake in a 450° oven for 15 to 20 minutes or till golden. Makes 4 servings.

LONDON BROIL

1 1- to 1¼-pound beef flank steak
¼ cup cooking oil
2 tablespoons red wine vinegar
1 small clove garlic, minced
   Freshly ground pepper

Score steak on both sides. Place in a plastic bag in a baking dish. Combine oil, vinegar, and garlic; pour over meat. Close bag. Let stand at room temperature 2 to 3 hours, turning several times. Remove meat; place on the rack of an unheated broiler pan. Broil 3 inches from heat 4 to 5 minutes. Sprinkle with pepper. Turn; broil 4 to 5 minutes more for medium-rare. Sprinkle with pepper. Slice into thin diagonal slices. Serves 5.

ROAST BEEF AU POIVRE

1 3-pound beef eye of round roast
1 small onion, sliced
1 cup dry red wine
1 tablespoon cracked pepper

Place roast and onion in a plastic bag in a baking dish; pour in wine. Close bag. Marinate in refrigerator overnight, turning bag occasionally. Drain meat, reserving onion and marinade.

Place onion on rack in roasting pan. Press pepper into surface of meat; place meat atop onion. Insert meat thermometer so bulb rests in center. Roast, uncovered, in a 325° oven about 1½ hours for medium (160°); spoon marinade over meat occasionally. Remove meat and onion from pan. Slice meat thinly. Skim fat from pan juices; spoon juices over meat. Serves 10.

After marinating the meat, press the cracked pepper into the surface of the meat so it's evenly distributed.

BEEF

BRISKET CARBONNADE

Braising the brisket in beer gives this dish its tenderness and robust flavor.

1   3- to 4-pound fresh beef brisket
3   medium onions, sliced
1   12-ounce can (1½ cups) beer
1   tablespoon brown sugar
½   teaspoon dried thyme, crushed
8   whole black peppercorns
2   bay leaves
2   cloves garlic, minced
¼   cup all-purpose flour

Trim excess fat from the meat. Place meat in a 13x9x2-inch baking dish; cover with the onions. Reserve ⅓ *cup* of the beer. Combine the remaining beer, sugar, thyme, peppercorns, bay leaves, and garlic. Pour over the meat. Cover tightly with foil. Bake in a 350° oven 3 to 3½ hours or till meat is tender. Transfer meat to a platter; keep warm. Skim the fat from pan juices; remove bay leaves.

For gravy, in a saucepan cook juices down to 1¾ cups, or add water if necessary to make 1¾ cups liquid. Blend reserved ⅓ cup beer into flour; stir into pan juices. Cook and stir till thickened and bubbly; cook and stir 1 minute more. Slice meat across grain; pass gravy. Makes 10 servings.

ITALIAN EGGPLANT BEEF STEW

1½ pounds beef stew meat, cut into
      1-inch cubes
2   tablespoons cooking oil
3   medium tomatoes, peeled and
      cut into wedges
1   cup chopped onion
2   tablespoons tomato paste
½   teaspoon dried oregano, crushed
½   teaspoon dried basil, crushed
½   teaspoon ground cumin
¼   to ½ teaspoon ground red
      pepper
2   cloves garlic, minced
1   cup water
1   large potato, peeled and cubed
      (1 cup)
1   cup dry white wine
2   cups coarsely chopped peeled
      eggplant
1   cup sliced fresh mushrooms
½   cup chopped green pepper

In a Dutch oven brown *half* of the beef at a time in hot oil; drain off fat. Return all meat to the Dutch oven. Add tomatoes, onion, tomato paste, oregano, basil, cumin, ground red pepper, and garlic. Stir in water. Bring to boiling; reduce heat. Simmer, covered, for 45 minutes. Add potato and wine; cover and simmer 10 minutes more. Stir in eggplant, mushrooms, and green pepper. Cover and simmer 15 to 20 minutes more or till meat and vegetables are tender. Makes 6 to 8 servings.

Pictured opposite: Italian Eggplant Beef Stew

Main Dishes
BEEF

SAVORY STEAK AND VEGETABLES

All the flavors of Swiss steak, minus the salt.

8 ounces boneless beef round steak, cut ½ inch thick
1 tablespoon cooking oil
1 cup water
½ of a 6-ounce can (⅓ cup) tomato paste
1 teaspoon Worcestershire sauce
¼ teaspoon dried basil, crushed
¼ teaspoon dried thyme, crushed
⅛ teaspoon dried marjoram, crushed
2 medium carrots, cut into strips
1 medium green pepper, cut into strips
½ cup sliced fresh mushrooms

Trim excess fat from round steak; cut steak into 2 portions. Sprinkle with pepper. In a 3-quart saucepan brown meat on both sides in hot cooking oil. Stir in water, tomato paste, Worcestershire sauce, basil, thyme, and marjoram. Bring to boiling; reduce heat. Cover and simmer for 30 minutes.

Add carrots; cover and simmer 15 minutes more. Add green pepper and mushrooms; cover and simmer about 10 minutes more or till meat and vegetables are tender. Transfer meat and vegetables to a serving platter. Spoon tomato mixture over. If desired, serve with hot cooked rice or noodles (cooked without salt). Makes 2 servings.

AUSTRIAN CARAWAY STEAK STRIPS

1 pound beef top round steak, cut into bite-size strips
1 cup chopped onion
½ cup thinly sliced carrot
1 clove garlic, minced
2 tablespoons cooking oil
½ cup dry white wine
⅓ cup water
½ teaspoon caraway seed
½ teaspoon dried marjoram, crushed
½ teaspoon dried thyme, crushed
⅛ teaspoon pepper
4 teaspoons all-purpose flour
¾ cup dairy sour cream
2 cups hot cooked noodles (cooked without salt)

In a skillet cook beef strips, onion, carrot, and garlic in hot oil till meat is brown and onion is tender. Stir in wine, water, caraway seed, marjoram, thyme, and pepper. Bring to boiling; reduce heat. Cover and simmer for 15 minutes.

Stir the flour into the sour cream; stir into beef mixture. Cook and stir till thickened, but *do not boil.* Serve over hot cooked noodles. Makes 4 servings.

ORIENTAL BEEF STIR-FRY

Sidestep salty soy sauce in this recipe with a unique combination of vinegar, sherry, and spices.

1 pound beef top round steak
1 tablespoon cornstarch
1 teaspoon sugar
½ teaspoon aniseed, crushed
¼ teaspoon garlic powder
⅓ cup dry sherry
¼ cup water
2 tablespoons vinegar
1 teaspoon Worcestershire sauce
2 tablespoons cooking oil
1½ cups broccoli, cut into ½-inch pieces
2 medium carrots, shredded
1 medium onion, cut into thin wedges
1 8-ounce can sliced water chestnuts, drained
1 cup sliced fresh mushrooms

Partially freeze round steak; slice very thinly into bite-size strips. Stir together the cornstarch, sugar, aniseed, and garlic powder. Stir in the sherry, water, vinegar, and Worcestershire sauce. Set aside.

Preheat a wok or large skillet over high heat; add oil. Stir-fry broccoli, carrots, and onion in hot oil about 3 minutes or till broccoli is crisp-tender. Remove from the wok. (Add more oil, if necessary.) Add *half* of the sliced beef to hot wok or skillet; stir-fry 2 to 3 minutes or till brown. Remove beef. Stir-fry remaining beef 2 to 3 minutes. Return all meat to wok. Add water chestnuts and mushrooms. Stir-fry for 1 minute.

Stir the cornstarch mixture; stir into wok. Cook and stir till thickened and bubbly. Return broccoli, carrots, and onion to wok; cover and cook about 2 minutes more or till heated through. Makes 6 servings.

DILLED BEEF STROGANOFF

¾ pound beef top round steak
1 tablespoon cooking oil
2 cups sliced fresh mushrooms
½ cup water
½ cup dry sherry
1 tablespoon tomato paste
1 8-ounce carton plain yogurt
1 tablespoon all-purpose flour
1 tablespoon sugar
1 teaspoon dried dillweed
Dash pepper
2 cups hot cooked rice (cooked without salt)

Trim fat from round steak. Partially freeze steak. Thinly slice into bite-size strips. In a large skillet brown meat, *half* at a time, in hot oil for 2 to 4 minutes. Remove meat from skillet. Add the sliced mushrooms; cook for 2 to 3 minutes or till tender. Remove mushrooms from skillet.

In a skillet stir together water, sherry, and tomato paste; bring to boiling. Cook, uncovered, over high heat about 3 minutes or till liquid is reduced to ⅓ cup; reduce heat. Combine yogurt, flour, sugar, dillweed, and pepper. Stir yogurt mixture into liquid in the skillet; stir in meat and mushrooms. Heat through over low heat till thickened but *do not boil.* Serve over hot cooked rice. Makes 4 servings.

TACO-STYLE SPUDS

Put the toppings in bowls on the table and let everyone top their own spud.

6 baking potatoes
1 pound ground beef
¼ cup shredded carrot
¼ cup sliced green onion
¾ cup water
½ of a 6-ounce can (⅓ cup) tomato paste
2 teaspoons chili powder
½ teaspoon dried oregano, crushed
⅛ teaspoon garlic powder
¾ cup shredded lettuce
¾ cup dairy sour cream
⅓ cup shredded cheddar cheese
Low-Sodium Taco Sauce (see recipe, page 12) *or* bottled hot pepper sauce

Prick potatoes with a fork. Bake in a 425° oven for 40 to 60 minutes or till tender. Meanwhile, in a 10-inch skillet cook ground beef, shredded carrot, and sliced green onion till meat is brown and vegetables are tender. Drain well. Stir in water, tomato paste, chili powder, oregano, and garlic powder. Bring to boiling; reduce heat. Cover and simmer for 15 minutes.

To assemble, gently roll each potato under your hand using a pot holder. Cut a crisscross in the top of each with a knife. Press ends and push up. Top each potato with some of the meat mixture. Garnish each with shredded lettuce, sour cream, and shredded cheddar cheese. Serve with Low-Sodium Taco Sauce or hot pepper sauce. Makes 6 servings.

SWEET AND SOUR CHILI

Whole kernel corn replaces the beans in this delightfully different chili.

1 pound lean ground beef
½ cup chopped onion
½ cup chopped green pepper
1 clove garlic, minced
1¾ cups water
1 10-ounce package frozen whole kernel corn
1 6-ounce can tomato paste
¼ cup vinegar
2 tablespoons sugar
1 teaspoon dried oregano, crushed
½ teaspoon ground cumin
¼ teaspoon ground red pepper

In a large saucepan cook ground beef, onion, green pepper, and garlic till meat is brown and vegetables are tender; drain off fat. Stir in water, frozen whole kernel corn, tomato paste, vinegar, sugar, oregano, cumin, and red pepper. Bring mixture to boiling; reduce heat. Cover and simmer for 30 minutes, stirring occasionally. Stir in additional water if mixture is too thick. Makes 5 or 6 servings.

Pictured opposite: Taco-Style Spuds, Low-Sodium Taco Sauce (see recipe, page 12)

Main Dishes
BEEF

COUNTRY MEAT LOAF WITH APPLE BUTTER SAUCE

1 beaten egg
1 small cooking apple
⅓ cup quick-cooking rolled oats
¼ cup sliced green onion
1 teaspoon grated lemon peel
¼ teaspoon ground allspice
1 pound lean ground beef *or* pork
⅔ cup apple butter
2 tablespoons lemon juice
2 teaspoons brown sugar

In a bowl combine egg and 2 tablespoons *water*. Peel and coarsely shred apple. Stir shredded apple, oats, green onion, lemon peel, allspice, and ¼ teaspoon *pepper* into egg mixture. Add ground meat; mix well. Shape mixture into a loaf about 8 inches by 4 inches; place in a shallow baking pan. Bake in a 350° oven for 45 minutes.

Meanwhile, for sauce stir together apple butter, lemon juice, and brown sugar. Drain meat. Spoon about *half* of the sauce over meat loaf. Bake about 15 minutes more or till done. Heat remaining sauce; serve with meat loaf. Makes 5 servings.

SPAGHETTI WITH MEAT SAUCE

1 pound ground beef
½ cup chopped onion
½ cup chopped green pepper
2 cloves garlic, minced
2 pounds tomatoes, peeled and chopped (6 medium)
1 6-ounce can tomato paste
½ cup dry red wine
½ cup water
2 teaspoons sugar
1½ teaspoons dried oregano, crushed
1 teaspoon dried basil, crushed
1 teaspoon dried thyme, crushed
½ teaspoon fennel seed, crushed
¼ teaspoon crushed red pepper
2 bay leaves
12 ounces spaghetti, cooked (without salt) and drained

In a 3-quart saucepan cook beef, onion, green pepper, and garlic till meat is brown; drain. Stir in remaining ingredients *except* spaghetti. Simmer, covered, 15 minutes. Uncover; simmer 45 minutes more or to desired consistency, stirring occasionally. Remove bay leaves. Serve over spaghetti. Serves 6.

Crush the fennel seed and other dried herbs with a mortar and pestle to release more of their flavor and aroma. Place a small amount at a time in the mortar, then crush against the bottom and sides of the bowl using the pestle.

ORANGE-VEGETABLE PORK ROAST

Pictured on page 15. Beef variation pictured on the front cover.

1 4-pound pork shoulder arm
   roast
2 tablespoons cooking oil
1 teaspoon finely shredded
   orange peel
2 cups orange juice
2 medium onions, quartered
¾ teaspoon fines herbes *or*
   Lemon Fines Herbes
   (see recipe, page 14)
1 bay leaf
3 medium sweet potatoes, peeled
   and quartered
2 cups fresh *or* one 10-ounce
   package frozen brussels
   sprouts
1 cup sliced fresh mushrooms
2 tablespoons cornstarch

Trim excess fat from meat. In a large Dutch oven heat cooking oil. Brown meat in hot oil. Spoon off fat. Add orange peel, orange juice, onions, fines herbes, and bay leaf. Bring to boiling; reduce heat. Simmer, covered, for 1 hour.

Add sweet potatoes. Cook for 20 minutes. Add brussels sprouts and mushrooms. Cook 15 to 20 minutes more or till meat and vegetables are tender. Transfer meat and vegetables to a warm serving platter. Keep warm.

For sauce, remove bay leaf from pan juices. Skim fat from juices. Reserve *2 cups* of the juices (add additional water, if needed). Combine cornstarch and ¼ cup *cold water*; stir into the reserved juices. Return to the Dutch oven. Cook and stir till thickened and bubbly. Cook and stir for 2 minutes more. Serve the sauce with meat and vegetables. Makes 8 servings.

• Orange-Vegetable Beef Roast • Prepare Orange-Vegetable Pork Roast as above, *except* substitute a 4-pound *beef chuck pot roast* for the pork shoulder arm roast.

BARBECUE-STYLE PORK SANDWICHES

Add the sodium figure for the homemade hamburger buns to the figure for this recipe to get the total sodium count per serving.

3 pounds boneless pork shoulder
   roast, cut into 1-inch pieces
3 cloves garlic, minced
1½ cups apple juice
1 large onion, chopped
1 6-ounce can tomato paste
2 tablespoons vinegar
2 teaspoons dry mustard
1 teaspoon dried marjoram,
   crushed
1 teaspoon paprika
½ teaspoon bottled hot
   pepper sauce
12 Hamburger Buns (see recipe,
   page 70) *or* 24 slices
   low-salt bread
1 cup finely shredded cabbage

In a saucepan bring meat, garlic, 2 cups *water,* and ¼ teaspoon *pepper* to boiling; reduce heat. Simmer, covered, about 1 hour or till meat is tender. Uncover; return to boiling. Cook for 30 to 40 minutes more or till most of the water is evaporated. Watch closely and stir mixture near the end so meat doesn't burn. Drain off fat. Using two forks, finely shred the cooked meat.

For sauce, in saucepan combine apple juice, onion, tomato paste, vinegar, mustard, marjoram, paprika, and hot pepper sauce. Bring to boiling; reduce heat. Simmer, covered, for 15 minutes. Stir shredded pork into mixture; heat through. Spoon the meat sauce onto hamburger buns or bread. Top with the finely shredded cabbage. Makes 12 servings.

PORK

PEACH-GLAZED PORK ROAST

Insert the meat thermometer so its bulb rests in the center of the meat's thickest portion. Be sure the bulb does not rest in fat or touch bone.

1 5-pound pork shoulder blade
   Boston roast
1 12-ounce jar peach preserves
¼ cup peach nectar
1 tablespoon lemon juice
¾ teaspoon ground allspice

Place meat on a rack in a shallow roasting pan. Insert the meat thermometer. Roast in a 325° oven for 2 to 3 hours or till the meat thermometer registers 130°.

Meanwhile, in a bowl combine the peach preserves, peach nectar, lemon juice, and allspice. Spoon half of the peach mixture over roast. Continue roasting about 45 minutes more or till the meat thermometer registers 170°. In a saucepan heat remaining peach mixture; pass with meat. Makes 10 servings.

SWEET AND SOUR PORK

Combining sweet and sour is a flavoring technique that tricks the palate and overrides the need for salt.

1 beaten egg
¼ cup cornstarch
¼ cup all-purpose flour
¼ cup dry sherry
1 pound boneless pork, cut into
   ¾-inch cubes
   Cooking oil for deep-fat frying
1 20-ounce can pineapple chunks
   (juice pack)
2 tablespoons cornstarch
1 cup water
¼ cup packed brown sugar
¼ cup red wine vinegar
2 tablespoons dry sherry
2 tablespoons cooking oil
1 medium green pepper, cut into
   1-inch pieces
1 medium carrot, thinly bias
   sliced
3 green onions, thinly sliced
2 cloves garlic, minced
1 teaspoon grated gingerroot

For batter, in a bowl combine egg, ¼ cup cornstarch, flour, and the ¼ cup dry sherry; beat till smooth. Dip pork cubes in batter. Fry in deep hot oil (365°) about 5 minutes or till golden. Drain; keep warm. Drain pineapple chunks, reserving ⅔ cup juice. Combine reserved pineapple juice and the 2 tablespoons cornstarch. Stir in water, brown sugar, red wine vinegar, and the 2 tablespoons sherry; set aside.

Preheat a wok or large skillet over high heat; add the 2 tablespoons cooking oil. Stir-fry the green pepper, carrot, green onions, garlic, and gingerroot in the hot oil for 2 to 3 minutes or till crisp-tender. Stir the vinegar mixture; stir into vegetables in the wok or skillet. Cook and stir till thickened and bubbly. Cook and stir 2 minutes more. Stir in the pork cubes and pineapple chunks. Heat through. Serve over hot cooked rice (cooked without salt), if desired. Makes 6 servings.

Pictured opposite: Sweet and Sour Pork

Main Dishes
PORK

PORK IN CIDER SAUCE

1 pound boneless pork, cut into bite-size strips
1 tablespoon cooking oil
½ cup apple cider *or* apple juice
¼ cup chopped onion
2 tablespoons brown sugar
4 teaspoons cornstarch
¼ teaspoon ground cinnamon
¼ teaspoon pepper
¼ cup apple cider *or* apple juice
3 tablespoons vinegar
1 tart medium cooking apple, cored and coarsely chopped
2 cups hot cooked noodles *or* hot cooked rice (cooked without salt)
2 tablespoons snipped parsley

In a 3-quart saucepan brown pork strips, half at a time, in hot cooking oil. Drain off fat. Return all meat to the saucepan. Add the ½ cup cider and the onion. Bring to boiling; reduce heat. Simmer, covered, about 40 minutes or till meat is tender.

In a bowl combine brown sugar, cornstarch, cinnamon, and pepper. Stir in the ¼ cup apple cider and the vinegar. Add to pork mixture. Stir in the coarsely chopped apple. Cook and stir till mixture is thickened and bubbly. Cook and stir 2 minutes more. Serve pork mixture over hot cooked noodles or rice. Garnish with the snipped parsley. Makes 4 servings.

CREOLE-STYLE LENTIL STEW

8 ounces boneless pork, cut into ½-inch cubes
1 large onion, chopped
2 cloves garlic, minced
1 tablespoon cooking oil
1 cup dry lentils
4 cups water
1 6-ounce can tomato paste
2 bay leaves
1 10-ounce package frozen cut okra, partially thawed
2 medium tomatoes, peeled and cut up
2 teaspoons Worcestershire sauce
1 teaspoon sugar
1 teaspoon dried oregano, crushed
½ teaspoon ground red pepper
1½ cups water
¾ cup long grain rice *or* bulgur wheat

In a 4-quart saucepan or Dutch oven cook pork cubes, onion, and garlic in hot cooking oil till meat is brown and onion is tender. Rinse the lentils. Stir the lentils, the 4 cups water, tomato paste, and bay leaves into the meat mixture. Bring mixture to boiling; reduce heat. Simmer, covered, for 30 minutes, stirring occasionally.

Stir in okra, tomatoes, Worcestershire sauce, sugar, oregano, and red pepper. Simmer, covered, about 30 minutes more or till okra and lentils are tender.

Meanwhile, in a saucepan combine the 1½ cups water and the rice or bulgur. Bring to boiling; reduce heat. Simmer, covered, about 15 minutes. To serve, ladle meat mixture into individual soup bowls. Mound the rice or bulgur wheat atop each serving. Makes 6 to 8 servings.

CURRIED PORK CHOP PLATTER

6 pork chops, cut ¾ inch thick
2 cups apple cider *or* apple juice
1 tablespoon curry powder
1 large onion, chopped
1 medium green pepper, cut
    into strips
½ cup chopped mixed dried fruits
    (3 ounces)
1½ cups ready-to-cook couscous *or*
    quick-cooking rice
3 tablespoons snipped parsley
½ teaspoon finely shredded
    lemon peel
2 tablespoons cornstarch
2 tablespoons cold water
    Chopped unsalted peanuts
    (optional)

Trim excess fat from chops. In a skillet cook fat trimmings till 2 tablespoons fat accumulate. Discard the trimmings. Brown chops slowly on both sides in hot fat. Remove chops; set aside. Add ½ *cup* of the apple cider or juice and the curry powder to the skillet. Cook over medium heat for 5 minutes, scraping up any browned bits off the bottom of the skillet.

Return chops to skillet. Add remaining apple cider or juice and onion. Simmer, covered, for 20 minutes. Add the green pepper and dried fruits. Simmer, covered, about 10 minutes more or till meat and vegetables are tender.

Meanwhile, prepare couscous or rice according to package directions, *except* omit salt. Stir parsley and lemon peel into cooked couscous or rice; spoon onto a large serving platter. Top with the chops; keep warm. Combine cornstarch and cold water; stir into fruit mixture. Cook and stir till thickened and bubbly. Cook and stir 2 minutes more. Spoon over chops. Sprinkle with peanuts, if desired. Makes 6 servings.

BRUNCH SANDWICHES

1 clove garlic, minced
½ teaspoon sugar
½ teaspoon dried rosemary,
    crushed
½ teaspoon fennel seed, crushed
½ teaspoon dry mustard
¼ teaspoon ground sage
¼ teaspoon pepper
⅛ teaspoon ground nutmeg
    Dash ground red pepper
1 pound ground pork
3 eggs
⅓ cup milk
¼ teaspoon ground cinnamon
12 slices French bread, cut
    ½ inch thick
    Cooking oil
1 cup chunk-style applesauce,
    heated
⅔ cup currant jelly, melted, *or*
    maple-flavored syrup

In a mixing bowl combine garlic, sugar, rosemary, fennel seed, dry mustard, sage, pepper, nutmeg, and red pepper.

Add the ground pork; mix well. Shape the meat mixture into 6 oval patties, ¼ to ⅜ inch thick. Preheat a large skillet. Cook the patties over medium heat about 10 minutes or till done, turning once. Drain patties; keep warm. Drain fat from skillet; wipe skillet with paper toweling.

In a shallow bowl beat together the eggs, milk, and ground cinnamon. Dip both sides of the bread slices in the egg mixture. In the skillet cook bread slices on both sides in a small amount of hot cooking oil over medium-high heat till golden brown. Add more cooking oil, if necessary.

To assemble sandwiches, place hot meat patties on 6 of the bread slices. Top patties with some of the warm applesauce and a second bread slice. Drizzle melted jelly or syrup over each sandwich. Makes 6 servings.

Main Dishes
PORK

STUFFED CABBAGE ROLLS

---

12 medium cabbage leaves *or* romaine leaves
1 cup water
1 beaten egg
¾ cup cooked rice (cooked without salt)
½ cup chopped onion
½ cup chopped tomato
½ teaspoon caraway seed, crushed
¼ teaspoon dried thyme, crushed
¼ teaspoon pepper
1 pound ground pork
1 tablespoon butter *or* margarine
1 tablespoon all-purpose flour
2 teaspoons Dijon-style mustard *or* Low-Sodium Dijon-Style Mustard (see recipe, page 11)
1 cup milk
¼ cup dairy sour cream
Paprika

Remove 2 inches of the heavy center vein of cabbage or romaine leaves, keeping each leaf in 1 piece. In a large saucepan or Dutch oven bring water to boiling. Add cabbage or romaine leaves. Cook, covered, for 2 to 3 minutes or till cabbage or romaine leaves are limp. Drain, reserving liquid.

In a large mixing bowl stir together the beaten egg, the cooked rice, chopped onion, chopped tomato, crushed caraway seed, the dried thyme, and the pepper. Stir in the ground pork; mix well.

Place about ¼ *cup* of the meat mixture in the center of each cabbage or romaine leaf; fold in sides. Starting at an unfolded edge, roll up each leaf, making sure folded sides are included in roll. Return to the saucepan or Dutch oven; add ¼ *cup* of the reserved liquid. Bring to boiling; reduce heat. Simmer, covered, for 35 minutes, adding more of the reserved liquid if necessary. Transfer cabbage rolls to a platter; keep warm.

For sauce, in a small saucepan melt butter or margarine. Stir in flour and mustard. Add milk all at once. Cook and stir till thickened and bubbly. Cook and stir 1 minute more. Stir in sour cream; heat through, but *do not boil.* Pour sauce over cabbage rolls. Sprinkle with paprika. Makes 6 servings.

To remove the heavy stem end from each cabbage or romaine leaf, cut along both sides of the center vein for about 2 inches.

SKILLET PIZZA FOR TWO

This robust-flavored pizza has a crispy whole wheat crust.

½ to ¾ cup all-purpose flour
½ cup whole wheat flour
1 package active dry yeast
½ cup warm water (115° to 120°)
1 tablespoon cooking oil
  Cornmeal
4 ounces ground pork
¼ cup chopped onion
1 clove garlic, minced
¼ cup water
3 tablespoons tomato paste
½ teaspoon dried basil, crushed
½ teaspoon dried oregano, crushed
¼ teaspoon sugar
¼ teaspoon fennel seed
⅛ teaspoon crushed red pepper
½ cup shredded mozzarella cheese
  (2 ounces)
½ small green pepper, sliced *or*
  chopped
¼ cup sliced fresh mushrooms

In a small mixer bowl combine ¼ *cup* of the all-purpose flour, the whole wheat flour, and the yeast. Stir in the warm water and oil. Beat with electric mixer on low speed for ½ minute, scraping the sides of the bowl constantly. Beat on high speed for 3 minutes. Stir in as much of the remaining all-purpose flour as you can mix in using a spoon. Turn out onto a lightly floured surface. Knead in enough of the remaining all-purpose flour to make a moderately stiff dough that is smooth and elastic (3 to 5 minutes total). Cover; let rest 10 minutes.

Grease a heavy 8-inch skillet that has an oven-proof handle; sprinkle a little cornmeal in bottom. With greased fingers, pat dough onto bottom and halfway up sides of skillet. Bake in a 375° oven for 15 to 20 minutes or till golden brown.

Meanwhile, for sauce, in a saucepan cook pork, onion, and garlic till meat is brown and onion is tender; drain. Stir in water, tomato paste, basil, oregano, sugar, fennel seed, and red pepper. Bring to boiling; reduce heat. Simmer, uncovered, for 4 minutes, stirring occasionally. Remove from heat.

Spoon sauce over hot baked crust. Top with cheese, green pepper, and mushrooms. Return to the 375° oven; bake about 15 minutes more or till cheese is bubbly. Makes 2 servings.

MOLASSES-SAUCED RIBS

3 cups water
1 large onion, finely chopped
1 6-ounce can tomato paste
⅓ cup molasses
2 tablespoons vinegar
4 cloves garlic, minced
2 bay leaves
2 teaspoons grated gingerroot *or*
  ½ teaspoon ground ginger
2 teaspoons dried basil, crushed
1 teaspoon dry mustard
1 teaspoon chili powder
½ teaspoon pepper
3 pounds pork loin back ribs, cut
  into 2-rib portions

For sauce, in a saucepan combine water, onion, tomato paste, molasses, vinegar, garlic, bay leaves, gingerroot, basil, dry mustard, chili powder, and pepper. Bring to boiling; reduce heat. Simmer, uncovered, about 30 minutes or till mixture is reduced to 2½ cups, stirring occasionally. Remove bay leaves.

Meanwhile, place the pork ribs, meaty side down, in a shallow roasting pan. Bake in a 450° oven for 30 minutes. Remove from the oven; drain off fat. Turn ribs meaty side up. Lower the oven temperature to 350°. Brush sauce over meat. Cover and bake in the 350° oven for 45 minutes. Uncover; bake for 15 minutes more, brushing sauce over meat occasionally. Refrigerate any leftover sauce. Makes 6 servings.

HERBS & SPICES

Use herbs and spices instead of salt to step up the flavor of your food. Start with ¼ teaspoon for each pound of meat, 2 cups of sauce, or 4 servings, and add more if you need it. Before using, snip fresh herbs or crush dried herbs. To substitute, use three times as much fresh herbs as you would dried herbs.

basil
Subtly sweet and somewhat minty, it's sometimes called the tomato herb because of its natural affinity for tomatoes. Add to tomato-sauced pasta dishes, meat loaf, green beans, peas, and squash. Good with pork, fish, or eggs.

bay leaves
Add one or two of these aromatic leaves to soups, stews, and pot roast at the beginning of cooking time. Slip one in when cooking new potatoes or rice pudding.

caraway seed
Famous for what it does for rye breads, this licorice-flavored seed adds an interesting background flavor to soups and stews, meats (especially pork), cabbage, carrots, cauliflower, potatoes, and noodles.

celery seed
Produced by a plant that's a relative of the green vegetable, this tiny seed lends a fresh celery flavor to salad dressings, pickles, coleslaw, vegetables, turkey stuffing, meat loaf, and fish. Try it in scrambled eggs.

cumin seed
Exotic, hot, and slightly bitter are the characteristics of cumin that make it a chief ingredient in chili powder and curry powder. Try it in salad dressings, spicy tomato sauces, meat loaf, bean dishes, eggs, and dips.

curry powder
A blend of 16 to 20 spices that gives distinction to meats, fish, poultry, vegetables, and fruits. A handy seasoning for egg dishes, rice, vegetables, salad dressings, and dips. Sprinkle it on unsalted nuts or popcorn instead of salt.

dill
Both dillseed and dillweed are very versatile, adding springtime flavor to meats, poultry, fish and seafood, vegetables, and eggs. Great in potato salad.

garlic
Use garlic in fresh or dried form, avoiding garlic salt. Use discreetly in meat, poultry, and seafood dishes as well as in vegetables, sauces, salad dressings, and marinades.

ginger
This spice's gentle bite makes it useful in main dishes (especially Oriental ones), vegetables, marinades, fruits, breads, and sweets. Available ground or as fresh gingerroot, which requires grating before use.

marjoram
This "herb of a thousand uses" is a mild cousin of oregano. It's a pleasant addition to casseroles, roasts, stews, vegetables, and salad dressings.

mint
The clean aroma and flavor of mint bring out the best in lamb, fruits, and beverages. A natural with peas or carrots.

mustard
Lively and pungent, dry mustard adds excitement to meat sauces, marinades, and salad dressings. Scatter mustard seed in pickles, relishes, or coleslaw.

oregano
Though nicknamed "the pizza herb," use of this robust herb should go beyond Italian dishes. It has a special flair with beef, and blends well in most meat, fish, poultry, egg, and vegetable dishes.

pepper
Its proven talent in flavoring all kinds of meat and vegetable dishes has made black pepper "the world's favorite spice."

red pepper
The pungency of red pepper makes it invaluable for seasoning, provided one uses it with respect. Add with restraint to meats, poultry, seafood, and eggs. A few dashes make an otherwise bland cream sauce or soup a lively one.

rosemary
These tiny pine-needlelike leaves release a bittersweet aroma and flavor when crushed. Rosemary blends well with other herbs, but it should be used sparingly because it is potent. Excellent with lamb, chicken, potatoes, and peas.

sage
Sage gives poultry stuffing its characteristic flavor. A wise choice for fish and vegetable chowders and for pork dishes in general.

sesame seed
Add to sweet and savory foods for a mild nutty flavor. Sprinkle on breads or casseroles before baking. Or, toast in the oven to bring out the flavor; then add to piecrusts, stuffings, meat loaves, salads, noodles, or vegetables.

tarragon
The sweet taste reminds some of licorice and mint. It tends to dominate other flavors, so add sparingly to chicken, fish, and delicate sauces.

thyme
This slightly pungent herb is one of the most popular because it blends well with so many foods and with other herbs. Use sparingly in chicken stews and casseroles, in fish soups, in cream sauces, and with tomato dishes. Stir into unsalted butter to serve over vegetables.

LAMB

LEMON-HERB LAMB CHOPS

To check the doneness of lamb chops, slit the center of a chop. If the inside color is pink, the chop is medium; if color is gray, the chop is well done.

4 lamb loin chops, cut 1 inch
  thick (1¼ pounds total)
2 small onions, thinly sliced
½ cup cooking oil
¼ cup lemon juice
2 tablespoons snipped parsley
1 clove garlic, minced
1 bay leaf, crushed
½ teaspoon dried oregano, crushed
¼ teaspoon pepper

Place lamb chops in an 8x8x2-inch baking pan; top with onion slices. For marinade, combine cooking oil, lemon juice, parsley, garlic, crushed bay leaf, oregano, and pepper. Pour marinade over chops. Cover and marinate in the refrigerator for 6 hours or overnight, turning chops several times.

Drain lamb chops; reserve marinade, if desired. Place chops on rack of an unheated broiler pan. Broil 3 inches from heat for 5 minutes. Turn chops; broil for 5 to 6 minutes more or to desired doneness. If you like, spoon *1 tablespoon* of the reserved marinade over *each* chop before serving. Makes 4 servings.

POCKET LAMB BURGERS

You get double mint flavor in these refreshing sandwiches—a little in the burger and a little in the vegetable-yogurt topper.

2 tablespoons plain yogurt
2 tablespoons thinly sliced
  green onion
1 teaspoon dried mint, crushed
½ teaspoon finely shredded
  lemon peel
⅛ teaspoon pepper
1 pound ground lamb
1 medium tomato, seeded and
  finely chopped
1 small cucumber, seeded and
  finely chopped
½ cup plain yogurt
½ teaspoon dried mint, crushed
6 small pita bread rounds *or* 3
  regular pita bread rounds,
  halved
6 lettuce leaves

Combine the 2 tablespoons yogurt, green onion, 1 teaspoon mint, lemon peel, and pepper; let stand 1 to 2 minutes. Add ground lamb; mix well. Shape meat mixture into six 3-inch-diameter patties. Place on the rack of an unheated broiler pan. Broil 3 inches from heat to desired doneness, turning once (allow 6 to 8 minutes total time for medium).

Meanwhile, stir together tomato, cucumber, the ½ cup plain yogurt, and the ½ teaspoon mint; set aside. For each sandwich, open a whole small pita round or a regular pita half to form a pocket. Place a lettuce leaf inside each pocket; insert a cooked meat patty. Top patty with some of the yogurt-tomato mixture; pass the remaining. Makes 6 servings.

POULTRY

SHERRY-BASTED CHICKEN WITH ORIENTAL STUFFING

*Another time, transform the stuffing into a pilaf. Prepare as directed below
except serve the rice mixture hot from the saucepan.*

1 cup quick-cooking brown rice
½ cup coarsely chopped walnuts
⅓ cup sliced green onion
1 teaspoon grated gingerroot
1 tablespoon butter *or* margarine
¼ cup snipped parsley
3 tablespoons dry sherry
1 3-pound whole roasting chicken
1 tablespoon butter *or* margarine
2 tablespoons dry sherry

For stuffing, in a 1½-quart saucepan cook brown rice according to package directions, *except* omit the salt. In a small skillet cook the chopped walnuts, sliced green onion, and gingerroot in 1 tablespoon butter or margarine till onion is tender. Stir snipped parsley, the 3 tablespoons dry sherry, and the walnut mixture into the cooked rice.

Rinse chicken and pat dry with paper toweling. Spoon some of the stuffing loosely into the neck cavity; pull the neck skin to the back of the bird and fasten securely with a small skewer. Lightly spoon remaining stuffing into the body cavity. (Bake any stuffing that does not fit in bird in a covered, small casserole during the last 25 to 30 minutes of roasting.) Twist wing tips under back. Place chicken, breast side up, on a rack in a shallow roasting pan. Melt 1 tablespoon butter or margarine; stir in the 2 tablespoons dry sherry. Brush skin of chicken with sherry mixture. Insert a meat thermometer into the center of the inside thigh muscle, making sure the bulb does not touch bone. Roast, uncovered, in a 375° oven for 1¼ to 1½ hours or till thermometer registers 180° to 185°, basting occasionally with drippings. Makes 6 servings.

LIME AND HONEY CHICKEN

You'll need two fresh limes to squeeze enough juice for the marinade.

¼ cup cooking oil
¼ cup lime juice
2 teaspoons snipped parsley
½ teaspoon dried oregano, crushed
¼ teaspoon paprika
1 small clove garlic, minced
1 2½- to 3-pound broiler-fryer
   chicken, cut up
1 tablespoon honey

For marinade, in a screw-top jar combine oil, lime juice, parsley, oregano, paprika, and garlic. Place chicken pieces in plastic bag; set in a shallow baking dish. Pour marinade over chicken; close the bag securely. Marinate in the refrigerator for 4 hours or overnight, turning occasionally. Drain, reserving marinade.

Place chicken pieces, skin side down, on the rack of an unheated broiler pan. Broil 5 to 7 inches from heat for 20 to 25 minutes. Stir honey into remaining marinade. Turn; broil 15 to 20 minutes more, brushing chicken pieces with honey-marinade mixture the last 5 minutes of broiling. Makes 6 servings.

POULTRY

SEASONED FRIED CHICKEN

*Pick whichever flavoring you want for fried chicken: basil, marjoram,
curry powder, poultry seasoning, or chili powder.*

1   2½- to 3-pound broiler-fryer
    chicken, cut up
3   tablespoons all-purpose flour
2   teaspoons dried basil, crushed;
    dried marjoram, crushed; curry
    powder; poultry seasoning; *or*
    chili powder
1   teaspoon paprika
½   teaspoon pepper
2   tablespoons cooking oil *or*
    shortening

Rinse chicken pieces; pat dry with paper toweling. In a plastic or paper bag combine flour, seasoning, paprika, and pepper. Add a few chicken pieces at a time; shake to coat.

In a 12-inch skillet heat cooking oil or shortening. Add chicken, placing meaty pieces toward center of skillet. Cook, uncovered, over medium heat for 10 to 15 minutes, turning to brown evenly. Reduce heat; cover tightly. Cook 30 minutes. Uncover; cook 10 to 15 minutes more, turning if necessary. Chicken is done when it is easily pierced with a fork. Drain chicken pieces on paper toweling. Makes 6 servings.

CHICKEN BREASTS À L'ORANGE

*Arrange the rice and chicken pieces as shown opposite on your prettiest platter for
an elegant and novel presentation.*

3   whole small chicken breasts
    (1½ pounds total), skinned,
    halved lengthwise, and boned
    Several dashes ground red
    pepper
1   small orange
1   cup regular *or* quick-cooking
    brown rice
¼   cup snipped parsley
½   teaspoon dried basil, crushed
2   tablespoons all-purpose flour
1   tablespoon sugar
1¼ cups orange juice
2   teaspoons aromatic bitters
    Parsley (optional)

Arrange chicken in a 12x7½x2-inch baking pan; sprinkle with the red pepper. Bake, covered, in a 350° oven for 25 minutes. Meanwhile, remove peel from the orange. Slice *half* of the peel into julienne strips; discard remaining peel. Simmer julienne strips in enough water to cover for 15 minutes; drain well and set aside. Section orange; set aside. Cook the brown rice according to package directions, *except* omit the salt. Add the snipped parsley and dried basil; toss to mix. Spoon rice mixture onto a platter; keep warm.

For sauce, in a small saucepan stir together flour and sugar. Stir in the orange juice. Cook and stir till thickened and bubbly. Stir in orange strips and bitters. Remove chicken from oven. Place chicken on a cutting board. Hold a sharp knife so the blade is at a 45-degree diagonal angle to the edge of meat. Slice each chicken breast against the grain of the meat, making slices that are 1½ to 2 inches apart. Reassemble each chicken breast and return to baking pan. Spoon sauce over the sliced chicken. Continue baking, uncovered, for 5 to 10 minutes more or till heated through. Arrange chicken slices on the brown rice mixture; spoon orange sauce from baking pan atop chicken. Garnish with reserved orange sections and additional parsley, if desired. Makes 6 servings.

Pictured opposite: Chicken Breasts à l'Orange

SESAME CHICKEN

*If you don't have a meat mallet, use the flat side of a chef's
knife to pound the chicken pieces.*

4　teaspoons sesame seed
1　whole medium chicken breast,
　　skinned, halved lengthwise,
　　and boned
1　tablespoon vinegar
2　teaspoons sugar
2　teaspoons dry sherry
1　teaspoon cooking oil
½　teaspoon grated gingerroot *or*
　　⅛ teaspoon ground ginger
½　teaspoon soy sauce *or* Low-
　　Sodium Soy Sauce (see recipe,
　　page 14)
　　Dash ground red pepper
1　clove garlic, minced

To toast sesame seed, spread evenly in an 8x8x2-inch baking pan. Toast in a 350° oven 12 to 15 minutes or till light brown, stirring occasionally. Remove from the oven; set aside. Meanwhile, place 1 chicken breast half between 2 pieces of clear plastic wrap. Working from center to edges, pound lightly with the flat or fine-toothed side of a meat mallet to ¼-inch thickness. Repeat with other chicken piece. For marinade, stir together vinegar, sugar, sherry, oil, gingerroot or ground ginger, soy sauce, red pepper, and garlic.

Remove sesame seed from the pan; set aside. Arrange chicken in the pan. Pour marinade over chicken; turn to coat. Cover and refrigerate several hours. Remove chicken from marinade; place on the rack of an unheated broiler pan. Brush with marinade. Broil 6 inches from heat about 4 minutes or till golden. Turn. Brush with marinade; sprinkle with the toasted sesame seed. Broil about 5 minutes more or till chicken is done. Garnish with sliced green onion, if desired. Serves 2.

CHICKEN PICCATA

*Sauté the seasoned, boned chicken breasts and make the delicate
lemon-wine sauce in the same skillet.*

3　tablespoons all-purpose flour
¼　teaspoon dried tarragon,
　　crushed
¼　teaspoon pepper
2　whole medium chicken breasts,
　　skinned, halved lengthwise,
　　and boned
1　tablespoon cooking oil
1　tablespoon butter *or* margarine
¼　cup sliced green onion
1　clove garlic, minced
½　cup dry white wine
½　teaspoon finely shredded lemon
　　peel (set aside)
1　tablespoon lemon juice
2　tablespoons snipped parsley

Combine flour, tarragon, and pepper. Place 1 chicken breast half between 2 pieces of clear plastic wrap. Working from the center to the edges, pound lightly with the flat or fine-toothed side of a meat mallet to ¼-inch thickness. Repeat with the remaining chicken pieces. Coat chicken pieces with flour mixture. In a 10-inch skillet heat cooking oil over medium-high heat. Add chicken; cook for 2 to 3 minutes on each side or till golden brown. Remove the skillet from heat. Transfer chicken pieces to a warm platter. Cover chicken; keep warm.

Add butter or margarine to the skillet; add green onion and garlic. Return to heat and cook till onion is tender but not brown. Add wine and lemon juice. Simmer, uncovered, for 3 to 4 minutes, scraping up any browned bits in the skillet. Spoon mixture over chicken. Sprinkle with parsley and lemon peel. Makes 4 servings.

HAWAIIAN CHICKEN ROLLS

2 whole large chicken breasts,
    skinned, halved lengthwise,
    and boned
⅓ cup crushed pineapple, drained
¼ cup unsalted chopped almonds,
    toasted
2 tablespoons sliced green onion
2 tablespoons snipped parsley
1 beaten egg yolk
1¼ cups bite-size shredded wheat
    squares, crushed
½ cup coconut

Place 1 chicken breast half between 2 pieces of clear plastic wrap. Working from the center to the edges, pound lightly with the flat or fine-toothed side of a meat mallet to ⅛-inch thickness. Repeat with remaining chicken pieces.

Combine pineapple, almonds, onion, and parsley; spoon some onto center of each chicken piece. Fold in 2 sides; fold over the other 2 sides to resemble a bundle. Press the ends to seal. Combine egg yolk and 1 tablespoon *water*. Combine crushed cereal and coconut. Dip chicken in egg mixture, then roll in cereal mixture. Place chicken, seam side down, in a lightly greased shallow baking pan. Bake in a 375° oven for 35 to 40 minutes or till tender; do not turn. Makes 4 servings.

CHICKEN IN HERBED YOGURT SAUCE

2 whole medium chicken breasts
½ cup plain yogurt
2 tablespoons all-purpose flour
½ cup milk
½ teaspoon dried marjoram,
    crushed
¼ teaspoon dried thyme, crushed
⅛ teaspoon garlic powder
⅛ teaspoon pepper

Halve chicken breasts lengthwise and remove bones, leaving skin on chicken. Place chicken, skin side down, in a cold skillet. Place over medium-low heat. Cook without turning for 5 to 10 minutes or till brown. Place chicken, skin side up, in a 10x6x2-inch baking dish. Bake, uncovered, in a 375° oven about 25 minutes or till done. Drain. Meanwhile, in saucepan combine yogurt and flour; add remaining ingredients. Cook and stir till thickened and bubbly; pour over chicken. Sprinkle with paprika, if desired. Bake 5 minutes more. Serves 4.

Flavoring with Citrus Fruits

Citrus fruits are among a salt-watcher's best friends. Their tangy juice and tart peel bring out flavors without running up the sodium tab. Try freshly grated orange peel in oil-and-vinegar dressing. Make dips with plain yogurt, lemon peel, and an herb. Spark marinades and barbecue sauces with citrus juices. At the table, replace the salt shaker with lemon wedges and give the entrée and vegetables a squirt of fresh citrus flavor.

PASTA WITH CHICKEN, ZUCCHINI, AND TOMATOES

Use freshly grated Parmesan cheese for more intense flavor.

  4 ounces linguine *or* spaghetti
  1 tablespoon cooking oil
  1 medium zucchini, cut into
      1½ x ¼ -inch strips
  ½ cup sliced fresh mushrooms
  ½ teaspoon dried basil, crushed
  1 clove garlic, minced
  1 cup cubed cooked chicken
  ½ cup light cream
  ⅛ teaspoon pepper
  6 cherry tomatoes, halved
  2 tablespoons grated Parmesan
      cheese

In a large saucepan cook linguine or spaghetti according to package directions, *except* omit salt. Meanwhile, in a skillet heat the cooking oil over medium-high heat. Add zucchini, mushrooms, basil, and garlic; cook and stir for 2 to 3 minutes or till zucchini is crisp-tender.

Drain pasta; return to saucepan. Stir in chicken, cream, pepper, and zucchini mixture; heat through. Add tomatoes and Parmesan cheese; toss. Serve immediately. Serves 2 or 3.

CHICKEN SALAD IN BEER PUFFS

  ⅓ cup dairy sour cream
  2 tablespoons mayonnaise *or*
      salad dressing *or* Low-Sodium
      Mayonnaise (see recipe, page 9)
  1 teaspoon prepared mustard
  ¼ teaspoon dried dillweed
  ⅛ teaspoon bottled hot pepper
      sauce
  1½ cups finely chopped cooked
      chicken
  ½ cup finely chopped mushrooms
  ¼ cup finely chopped celery
  2 tablespoons sliced green onion
  ¼ cup shortening
  ⅓ cup beer
  ½ cup all-purpose flour
  2 eggs

In a bowl stir together sour cream, mayonnaise, mustard, dillweed, and hot pepper sauce. Stir in chicken, mushrooms, celery, and onion. Cover and chill.

In a medium saucepan melt shortening. Add beer; bring to boiling. Add flour all at once; stir vigorously. Cook and stir till mixture forms a ball that doesn't separate. Remove from heat; cool slightly (about 5 minutes). Add eggs, 1 at a time, beating with a wooden spoon 1 to 2 minutes after each or till smooth.

Drop by heaping tablespoonfuls into 5 mounds, 3 inches apart, onto a lightly greased baking sheet. Bake in a 400° oven for 25 to 30 minutes or till puffed and golden. Split puffs, removing any soft dough inside. Cool on a wire rack. To serve, fill puffs with chicken mixture. Makes 5 servings.

• **Chicken Salad Appetizer Puffs** • Prepare Chicken Salad in Beer Puffs as directed above, *except* drop the puff mixture by rounded teaspoonfuls 1 inch apart onto a lightly greased baking sheet. Bake in a 400° oven about 20 minutes. Split, cool, and fill as above. Makes 22 appetizers.

Pictured opposite: Pasta with Chicken,
Zucchini, and Tomatoes

MainDishes
POULTRY

CHICKEN AND VEGETABLES IN ORANGE SAUCE

*This stir-fry dish is pleasing to the eye as well as the palate. For even more flavor,
try it with a few drops of Low-Sodium Soy Sauce (see recipe, page 14).*

1 **whole medium chicken breast,
   skinned, halved lengthwise,
   and boned**
1 **teaspoon finely shredded
   orange peel**
⅔ **cup orange juice**
2 **teaspoons molasses**
2 **teaspoons cornstarch**
1 **medium carrot, roll-cut ¾ inch
   thick (see photo below)** *or* **bias-
   sliced ¼ inch thick**
2 **tablespoons cooking oil**
2 **teaspoons grated gingerroot** *or*
   ½ teaspoon ground ginger
1 **clove garlic, minced**
1 **cup sliced cauliflower flowerets**
½ **of a 6-ounce package frozen pea
   pods, thawed**
1 **cup hot cooked rice (cooked
   without salt)**

Cut chicken breast halves into 1-inch pieces. Stir orange peel, orange juice, and molasses into cornstarch; set aside. If using a roll-cut carrot, blanch the carrot pieces by cooking, covered, in boiling water for 5 minutes; drain.

Preheat a wok or large skillet over high heat; add cooking oil. Stir-fry gingerroot or ground ginger and garlic in hot oil for 30 seconds. Add sliced cauliflower and carrot, and stir-fry 2 minutes; remove from the wok. Add thawed pea pods and stir-fry 1 minute; remove from the wok. Add more oil to the wok, if needed. Stir-fry chicken 2 to 3 minutes or till done.

Stir the cornstarch mixture; stir into chicken in the wok. Cook and stir till thickened and bubbly. Stir in the stir-fried vegetables; cover and cook 1 to 2 minutes more. Serve over hot cooked rice. Makes 2 servings.

To roll-cut a carrot, make the first slice with the knife at an angle. Keeping the knife at the same angle, give the carrot a half-turn and make another slice about ¾ inch from the cut end. Continue with the rest of the carrot.

TURKEY CURRY

To toast coconut for topping the curry, spread a thin layer of coconut in a shallow baking pan. Toast in a 350° oven for 6 to 7 minutes or till it's lightly browned. Stir the coconut once or twice during toasting for even browning.

2 tablespoons cooking oil
1 medium cooking apple, peeled, cored, and chopped
½ cup chopped onion
2 to 3 teaspoons curry powder
1 clove garlic, minced
2 8-ounce cartons plain yogurt
4 teaspoons all-purpose flour
3 cups chopped cooked turkey
⅓ cup raisins
3 cups hot cooked rice (cooked without salt)
Sliced green onion (optional)
Unsalted peanuts (optional)
Toasted coconut (optional)

In a skillet heat cooking oil over medium-high heat. Cook apple, onion, curry powder, and garlic in hot oil till onion is tender. Remove from heat. Stir yogurt into flour; stir into onion mixture. Cook and stir over medium heat till mixture is thickened and bubbly. Stir in turkey and raisins; cook just till heated through *(do not boil)*. Serve over hot cooked rice. Garnish with sliced green onion, unsalted peanuts, and toasted coconut, if desired. Makes 6 servings.

WALDORF TURKEY TOSS WITH APPLE DRESSING

Try the dressing on fruit salads, too!

½ cup applesauce
⅓ cup honey
3 tablespoons vinegar
1 teaspoon poppy seed
½ teaspoon paprika
½ teaspoon finely shredded lemon peel
½ cup salad oil
3 cups torn mixed salad greens
2 cups cubed cooked turkey
2 medium apples, cored and chopped
½ cup broken walnuts

For dressing, in a small mixer bowl combine the applesauce, honey, vinegar, poppy seed, paprika, and lemon peel. Gradually add oil, beating constantly with an electric mixer till slightly thickened. Cover and chill.

In a salad bowl combine mixed greens, turkey, apples, and walnuts. Stir dressing; pour desired amount over salad and toss lightly. Store any remaining dressing, covered, in the refrigerator. Makes 4 servings.

FISH NEWBURG IN CHIVE CREPES

¾ cup all-purpose flour
¾ cup milk
⅓ cup water
1 egg
2 teaspoons cooking oil
1 teaspoon vinegar
¼ cup snipped chives *or* green onion tops
2 tablespoons butter *or* margarine
¼ cup chopped fresh mushrooms
2 tablespoons all-purpose flour
⅛ teaspoon pepper
⅛ teaspoon ground red pepper
1¾ cups light cream
2 beaten egg yolks
3 tablespoons dry white wine *or* dry sherry
1 tablespoon lemon juice
12 ounces fresh *or* frozen cod, cooked without salt, drained, and flaked (about 1½ cups)

In a bowl combine ¾ cup flour, the milk, water, egg, oil, and vinegar; beat with a rotary beater till blended. Stir in chives or green onion tops. Heat a lightly greased 6-inch skillet; remove from heat. Spoon in about 2 tablespoons batter; lift and tilt skillet to spread batter. Return to heat; brown on one side only. (*Or,* cook on an inverted crepe pan.) Invert the pan over paper toweling to remove crepe. Repeat to make 12 crepes, greasing the skillet occasionally.

For sauce, in a saucepan melt butter or margarine. Add mushrooms and cook till tender. Stir in 2 tablespoons flour, pepper, and red pepper. Add cream all at once. Cook and stir till thickened and bubbly. Stir about half of the hot mixture into egg yolks; return all to the saucepan. Cook and stir till thickened and bubbly. Stir in wine and lemon juice.

Stir *¾ cup* of the sauce into cooked fish; set remaining sauce aside. Spoon about 2 tablespoons of the fish mixture onto the unbrowned side of each crepe toward 1 edge; roll up crepe. Arrange in a 13x9x2-inch baking dish. Cover and bake in a 350° oven for 20 minutes. Uncover and drizzle remaining sauce over crepes; bake for 5 minutes more. If desired, garnish crepes with additional fresh chives or sprinkle with paprika. Makes 6 servings.

TARRAGON-MUSTARD HALIBUT STEAKS

Make any white fish steaks or fillets a sophisticated dish with this tasteful blend of wine, mustard, tarragon, and fresh mushrooms.

1½ pounds fresh *or* frozen halibut steaks
½ cup dry white wine
1 tablespoon Dijon-style mustard *or* Low-Sodium Dijon-Style Mustard (see recipe, page 11)
½ teaspoon dried tarragon, crushed
1½ cups sliced fresh mushrooms
2 tablespoons cooking oil
Parsley sprigs (optional)

Thaw fish, if frozen. Place fish in a 12x7½x2-inch baking dish. Stir together the wine, mustard, and tarragon; pour over fish. Bake, uncovered, in a 400° oven for 20 to 25 minutes or till fish flakes easily when tested with a fork. Transfer fish to a serving platter, reserving the juices.

Meanwhile, in a skillet cook mushrooms in hot oil till tender. Remove from heat. Strain fish juices; stir mushrooms into juices and spoon atop fish. If desired, garnish with parsley sprigs. Makes 6 servings.

Pictured opposite: Fish Newburg in Chive Crepes

MainDishes
FISH

WESTERN-STYLE BAKED FISH

1 **pound fresh *or* frozen cod fillets**
1 **large tomato**
3 **tablespoons finely chopped green pepper**
2 **tablespoons finely chopped onion**
¼ **cup dry bread crumbs (1 slice)**
½ **teaspoon dried basil, crushed**
1 **tablespoon cooking oil**

Thaw fish, if frozen. Place fish in a greased 10x6x2-inch baking dish; sprinkle with pepper. Slice tomato into ¼-inch-thick slices; arrange atop fish. Sprinkle with green pepper and onion. Combine bread crumbs and basil; toss with oil. Spread over tomatoes. Bake, uncovered, in a 350° oven about 25 minutes or till fish flakes easily when tested with a fork. Transfer to a serving platter. Makes 4 servings.

SKEWERED FISH AND VEGETABLES

⅓ **cup cooking oil**
¼ **cup lemon juice**
1 **teaspoon dried dillweed**
¾ **teaspoon dried tarragon, crushed**
2 **cloves garlic, minced**
1 **pound fresh *or* frozen haddock fillets, cut into 1-inch cubes**
2 **medium zucchini, cut diagonally into ½-inch pieces**
18 **cherry tomatoes**

In a bowl combine oil, lemon juice, dillweed, tarragon, and garlic. Add fish, stirring gently to coat. Cover and marinate at room temperature for 1 hour. Drain, reserving marinade.

On 6 skewers alternately thread fish and zucchini, leaving room at end of each for 3 tomatoes. Grill over *medium* coals (or broil 4 inches from heat) for 12 to 15 minutes or till fish flakes easily; turn and baste often with marinade. Add 3 tomatoes to each skewer during the last half of the cooking time. Serves 6.

To make peeling a garlic clove easier, first crush the clove using the flat side of a chef's knife. This loosens the skin so you can pull it off with your fingers.

BROILED FISH WITH TROPICAL TARTAR SAUCE

*Crushed pineapple plus the pulp of an entire lemon give
the tartar sauce its refreshing flavor.*

2 pounds fresh *or* frozen cod,
   haddock, *or* perch fillets
1 8-ounce can crushed pineapple
   (juice pack)
1 8-ounce carton dairy sour cream
1 small lemon, peeled, sectioned,
   and finely chopped
¼ cup finely chopped green
   pepper
2 tablespoons finely chopped
   onion
2 tablespoons milk
½ teaspoon celery seed
¼ teaspoon dry mustard
1 tablespoon cooking oil

Thaw fish, if frozen. Drain pineapple, reserving ¼ *cup* of the juice. For tartar sauce, in a small mixing bowl combine sour cream, lemon, green pepper, onion, milk, celery seed, dry mustard, and the drained pineapple; mix well. Cover and chill.

Preheat the broiler. Cut fillets into 6 portions. In a shallow dish combine oil and the ¼ cup reserved pineapple juice. Dip fish portions into mixture, turning to coat. Place fish on the rack of an unheated broiler pan. Broil 4 inches from heat till fish flakes easily when tested with a fork. Allow about 10 minutes for 1-inch-thick fish portions, turning halfway through cooking time. Serve with tartar sauce. Store any remaining sauce in the refrigerator. Makes 6 servings.

CREOLE SHRIMP AND CHICKEN

1 medium green pepper, chopped
1 medium onion, chopped
1 tablespoon cooking oil
5 medium tomatoes, peeled and
   chopped
½ teaspoon chili powder
¼ teaspoon ground red pepper
⅛ teaspoon garlic powder
⅛ teaspoon pepper
1 12-ounce package frozen
   shelled shrimp, thawed
1 cup cubed cooked chicken
2 cups hot cooked rice (cooked
   without salt)

In a skillet cook green pepper and onion in hot oil till tender but not brown. Stir in tomatoes, chili powder, red pepper, garlic powder, and pepper. Bring to boiling; reduce heat. Simmer, uncovered, for 20 to 30 minutes or till very thick. (Mixture will thin when shrimp is added.)

Stir in shrimp and chicken. Return to boiling; reduce heat and cook about 1 minute more or till shrimp turn pink. Serve over hot cooked rice. Makes 4 servings.

MEATLESS

ZUCCHINI-RICE PIE

Serve this quiche-like entrée with a fruit salad for a light lunch or brunch.

1 large onion, finely chopped
1 cup chopped fresh mushrooms
1 medium zucchini, chopped
    (1 cup)
½ teaspoon dried basil, crushed
½ teaspoon dried oregano, crushed
2 tablespoons butter *or* margarine
1½ cups cooked rice (cooked
    without salt)
5 beaten eggs
⅓ cup milk
¼ cup grated Parmesan cheese

In a saucepan cook onion, mushrooms, zucchini, basil, and oregano in butter or margarine till vegetables are tender but not brown. Stir in rice, eggs, milk, and *2 tablespoons* of the cheese. Turn into a well-greased 9-inch pie plate. Sprinkle with the remaining Parmesan cheese. Bake, uncovered, in a 350° oven for 25 to 30 minutes or till set. Let stand 10 minutes. Garnish with a halved cherry tomato and parsley, if desired. Makes 5 servings.

HEARTY VEGETABLE STEW

Cut the salt in this recipe even more by using one or more "low-salt" or "no-salt-added" canned products.

2 16-ounce cans tomatoes, cut up
1 15½-ounce can red kidney
    beans
1 15-ounce can great northern
    beans
1 15-ounce can garbanzo beans
3 medium onions, chopped
    (1½ cups)
2 medium green peppers,
    chopped (1½ cups)
2 stalks celery, sliced (1 cup)
1 medium yellow summer squash
    or zucchini, halved lengthwise
    and sliced (1 cup)
½ cup water
2 teaspoons chili powder
1½ teaspoons dried basil, crushed
¼ teaspoon pepper
2 cloves garlic, minced
1 bay leaf
1 cup unsalted peanuts *or*
    unsalted cashews

In a 4-quart Dutch oven combine *undrained* tomatoes, *undrained* beans, onions, green peppers, celery, squash, water, chili powder, basil, pepper, garlic, and bay leaf. Bring to boiling; reduce heat. Cover and simmer 1 hour. Stir in peanuts or cashews; heat through. Remove bay leaf. Makes 10 servings.

Pictured opposite: Hearty Vegetable Stew

Main Dishes
MEATLESS

CALIFORNIA OMELET

---

1 cup sliced fresh mushrooms
¼ cup chopped green pepper
3 tablespoons sliced green onion
2 teaspoons butter *or* margarine
4 eggs
2 tablespoons water
½ teaspoon dried chervil *or* tarragon, crushed
¼ teaspoon pepper
2 teaspoons butter *or* margarine
½ cup fresh alfalfa sprouts
¼ avocado, peeled and sliced
2 slices tomato, halved

In a skillet cook mushrooms, green pepper, and onion in 2 teaspoons butter about 3 minutes or till tender. Drain. Remove and keep warm. In a bowl combine eggs, water, chervil or tarragon, and pepper; beat with a fork till well blended.

In a 10-inch skillet with flared sides heat 2 teaspoons butter, lifting and tilting pan to coat sides. Add egg mixture; cook over medium heat. As eggs set, run a spatula around the edge of the skillet, lifting eggs to allow uncooked portion to flow underneath. When eggs are set but still shiny, remove from heat. Spoon mushroom mixture across center of omelet. Fold ⅓ of the omelet over the mixture. Fold the opposite ⅓ over all. Slide omelet out onto a warm platter. Top with alfalfa sprouts, avocado, and tomato. Makes 2 servings.

VEGETABLE LASAGNA

---

2 medium carrots, finely chopped
½ cup chopped onion
2 cloves garlic, minced
2 tablespoons olive oil *or* cooking oil
1 pound fresh tomatoes, cut up (3 medium)
1 6-ounce can tomato paste
½ cup water
1 teaspoon dried oregano, crushed
1 teaspoon dried basil, crushed
½ teaspoon dried thyme, crushed
¼ teaspoon pepper
2 bay leaves
1 cup sliced fresh mushrooms
1 8-ounce package whole wheat *or* regular lasagna noodles
1 10-ounce package frozen chopped spinach, thawed and well drained
1 beaten egg
2 cups cream-style cottage cheese, drained
1 cup shredded *or* crumbled farmer cheese

In a large saucepan cook carrots, onion, and garlic in hot oil till tender. Add tomatoes, tomato paste, and water; mix well. Stir in oregano, basil, thyme, pepper, and bay leaves. Bring to boiling; reduce heat. Simmer, uncovered, for 15 minutes. Stir in mushrooms; cook about 5 minutes more or till mixture is reduced to 3¼ cups. Remove from heat; discard bay leaves.

Meanwhile, cook lasagna noodles according to the package directions, *except* omit salt; drain well. Using paper toweling, squeeze any excess moisture from spinach. Combine egg and the drained cottage cheese.

In a 12x7½x2-inch baking dish layer ⅓ of the lasagna noodles, ⅓ of the spinach, ⅓ of the cottage cheese mixture, and ⅓ of the tomato mixture. Sprinkle with ⅓ of the farmer cheese. Repeat layers 2 more times. Cover with foil. Bake in a 375° oven for 40 minutes; remove foil and bake 10 minutes more. Remove from the oven; let stand 10 minutes before serving. Makes 8 to 10 servings.

Pictured opposite: Ratatouille-Topped Pasta (see recipe, page 60) and Herbed French Bread (see recipe, page 69)

Side Dishes

SIDE DISHES	Per Serving						Percent U.S. RDA Per Serving							
	SODIUM (mg)	Calories	Protein (g)	Carbohydrate (g)	Fat (g)	Potassium (mg)	Protein	Vitamin A	Vitamin C	Thiamine	Riboflavin	Niacin	Calcium	Iron
VEGETABLES														
Creamy Corn and Mushrooms (p. 55)	60	176	6	25	7	355	10	15	19	11	16	12	7	6
Creamy Winter Vegetable Soup (p. 57)	27	142	4	18	7	468	6	34	28	8	9	6	7	4
Gazpacho (p. 56)	13	115	2	12	7	529	4	34	91	9	5	7	3	8
Glazed Carrots, Apples, and Nuts (p. 59)	26	68	2	11	3	261	2	120	25	4	2	2	2	4
Green Beans Vinaigrette (p. 55)	15	59	1	7	3	164	2	8	13	3	4	2	3	3
Lemon Broccoli (p. 56)	17	128	4	7	11	444	6	57	219	8	15	5	12	7
Orange-and-Honey-Glazed Squash (p. 59)	3	149	4	38	0	895	5	53	77	9	15	7	7	11
Potato Pancakes with Applesauce Yogurt (p. 57)	33	204	6	31	7	653	9	4	52	13	9	11	5	8
Zucchini-Carrot Stir-Fry (p. 59)	15	53	1	5	3	215	2	67	21	3	4	4	3	2
RICE AND PASTA														
Curried Rice and Vegetables (p. 60)	9	144	3	17	8	175	5	4	16	8	3	10	2	5
Herbed Broccoli-Pasta Toss (p. 61)	28	185	6	28	6	257	10	19	58	20	15	10	9	7
Pasta with Parsley Pesto (p. 61)	16	159	5	22	6	113	7	10	16	18	8	9	4	7
Ratatouille-Topped Pasta (p. 60)	19	196	7	31	5	514	10	25	96	25	14	16	6	12
SALADS														
Avocado-Citrus Salad (p. 66)	8	287	3	25	22	745	4	11	118	12	11	8	4	8
Cucumber-Topped Tossed Salad (p. 65)	22	66	2	6	4	297	3	30	45	5	5	3	5	7
Fruit-and-Nut Spaghetti Squash Salad (p. 64)	27	220	4	28	12	742	7	37	72	17	11	7	8	12
Hot Potato Salad (p. 64)	4	124	3	24	2	490	4	5	44	9	3	9	1	5
Sweet-Sour Curry Dressing (p. 66)	0	94	0	9	7	13	0	0	2	0	0	0	0	0
Tabouleh (p. 62)	5	131	3	19	6	179	5	13	27	6	3	6	2	7
Tropical Fruit Salad (p. 66)	3	209	1	38	7	387	2	6	61	9	4	3	4	5
Vegetable-Nut Slaw (p. 65)	21	180	3	7	17	208	5	22	35	4	3	2	2	7
Vegetable Salad Shells (p. 62)	30	341	9	55	10	239	14	49	15	38	15	20	3	14
BREADS														
Cinnamon-Orange Popovers (p. 72)	41	168	6	20	7	103	9	5	2	12	12	6	6	6
Cinnamon-Raisin English Muffins (p. 71)	51	247	6	48	3	171	10	1	0	24	17	15	4	11
Dinner Rolls (p. 70)	37	126	3	21	4	35	5	3	0	11	7	7	1	5
English Muffins (p. 71)	56	253	7	47	4	107	11	1	0	27	19	17	3	10
Featherlight Pancakes (p. 72)	21	56	3	7	2	36	4	3	0	4	5	2	2	3
Hamburger Buns (p. 70)	73	252	6	41	7	69	10	6	0	21	14	13	1	9
Herbed French Bread (p. 69)	38	85	3	18	0	33	4	0	0	10	7	7	0	4
Honey-Wheat Bread (p. 69)	16	81	2	15	2	40	3	1	0	7	4	5	0	3
White Bread (p. 67)	34	88	3	17	1	36	4	0	0	9	6	6	1	4
Yeast Biscuits (p. 70)	18	174	3	19	10	43	4	0	0	11	8	7	1	4

CREAMY CORN AND MUSHROOMS

2 10-ounce packages frozen
   whole kernel corn
1½ cups thinly sliced mushrooms
½ cup thinly sliced green onion
2 tablespoons all-purpose flour
¼ teaspoon dried thyme, crushed
⅛ teaspoon pepper
1 cup milk
1 3-ounce package cream cheese,
   cut up

In a 3-quart saucepan cook corn, mushrooms, and green onion, covered, in a small amount of boiling water for 5 to 7 minutes or till vegetables are tender. Drain well.

Meanwhile, in a medium saucepan combine flour, thyme, and pepper; stir in milk. Cook and stir till thickened and bubbly. Cook and stir 1 minute more. Stir in cream cheese; cook and stir just till melted. Stir in drained vegetables; heat through. Makes 6 servings.

GREEN BEANS VINAIGRETTE

Try the tangy dill dressing over other hot cooked vegetables, too.

1 9-ounce package frozen cut
   green beans
1 stalk celery, sliced
1 small onion, cut into thin
   wedges
1 tablespoon cooking oil
1 teaspoon mustard seed
2 tablespoons vinegar
1 teaspoon sugar
¼ teaspoon dillweed

In a saucepan bring ⅓ cup *water* to boiling; stir in beans, celery, and onion. Return to boiling; reduce heat. Cover and simmer for 6 to 8 minutes or just till vegetables are tender; drain.

Meanwhile, in a skillet heat cooking oil over medium-high heat. Stir in mustard seed. Cover and heat till seed pops and turns grayish brown, stirring often. Remove from heat; stir in vinegar, sugar, and dillweed. Place the drained vegetables in a serving bowl. Pour vinegar mixture over vegetables. Toss and serve at once. Makes 4 servings.

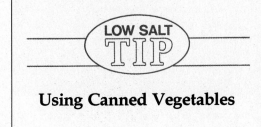

LOW SALT TIP
Using Canned Vegetables

A standard can of vegetables may have more than 100 times the sodium its raw or frozen counterpart cooked without salt has. One way to keep salt down and still enjoy the convenience of canned vegetables is to use "no-salt-added" or "low-salt" products. Another is to rinse the food with tap water. By rinsing canned vegetables and meats in a colander under running water for one minute, you can cut the sodium content significantly. It's easy and it works!

VEGETABLES

LEMON BROCCOLI

1 pound fresh broccoli
3 tablespoons cooking oil
2 tablespoons lemon juice
½ teaspoon dried oregano, crushed
⅛ teaspoon dry mustard
⅛ teaspoon pepper

Wash and trim broccoli; cut into stalks. Cook, covered, in boiling water for 10 to 12 minutes or till tender. Meanwhile, in a screw-top jar combine oil, lemon juice, oregano, dry mustard, and pepper; shake well. Drain the broccoli well; place in a serving bowl. Shake lemon mixture and pour over broccoli. Serve at once. Makes 4 servings.

GAZPACHO

3 large tomatoes (1¼ pounds)
¾ cup water
3 tablespoons tomato paste
½ medium cucumber, peeled, seeded, and chopped
¼ cup chopped green pepper
3 tablespoons chopped onion
2 tablespoons olive oil *or* cooking oil
2 tablespoons red wine vinegar
½ teaspoon sugar
⅛ teaspoon pepper
  Few drops bottled hot pepper sauce
1 small clove garlic, minced
  Whole green onions, unsalted breadsticks, *or* dairy sour cream

Peel tomatoes (see tip below). Core and coarsely chop tomatoes; measure about 3 cups. In a mixing bowl stir together water and tomato paste. Stir in chopped tomatoes, cucumber, green pepper, onion, oil, vinegar, sugar, pepper, hot pepper sauce, and garlic. Cover and chill. To serve, pour into chilled mugs; garnish each with a green onion, unsalted breadstick, or dollop of sour cream. Makes 4 to 6 servings.

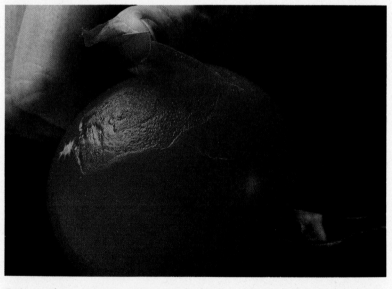

Before peeling a tomato, spear it with a fork and plunge it into boiling water for 30 seconds; immediately immerse in cold water. This loosens the skin for easier peeling.

CREAMY WINTER VEGETABLE SOUP

2 cups chopped peeled potatoes
2 cups chopped peeled winter
    squash (butternut, acorn,
    banana, *or* buttercup)
1¼ cups water
½ cup chopped onion
¼ cup snipped parsley
2 teaspoons dry mustard
1 teaspoon finely shredded
    lemon peel
½ teaspoon dried dillweed
¼ teaspoon pepper
2 cloves garlic, minced
1¼ cups light cream *or* milk
3 tablespoons unsalted sunflower
    nuts

In a large saucepan combine potatoes, squash, water, onion, parsley, dry mustard, lemon peel, dillweed, pepper, and garlic. Bring to boiling; reduce heat. Cover and simmer about 20 minutes or till vegetables are tender.

Transfer about 2 cups of the vegetable mixture to a blender container or food processor bowl. Cover; process till smooth. Return pureed mixture to vegetable mixture in the saucepan. Stir in light cream or milk; heat through. To serve, ladle into bowls; sprinkle unsalted sunflower nuts atop each serving. Makes 6 to 8 servings.

POTATO PANCAKES WITH APPLESAUCE YOGURT

Caraway seed in the pancakes and a topping of applesauce-sweetened yogurt give this side dish a German flavor. Ideal for a light supper or brunch.

1½ cups finely shredded potatoes
    (3 medium)
2 green onions, thinly sliced
1 beaten egg
1 tablespoon all-purpose flour
½ teaspoon dry mustard
¼ teaspoon caraway seed
⅛ teaspoon pepper
1 tablespoon cooking oil
⅓ cup applesauce
¼ cup plain yogurt
1 green onion, thinly sliced
    (optional)

In a mixing bowl stir together potatoes, two thinly sliced green onions, the egg, flour, dry mustard, caraway seed, and pepper; mix well. In a skillet heat oil over medium-high heat. For each pancake, pour about ¼ *cup* potato mixture into the skillet; spread batter slightly. Fry potato pancakes 3 or 4 minutes per side or till brown. Keep pancakes warm as more are fried.

Stir together applesauce, yogurt, and, if desired, one sliced green onion just till mixture is swirled; serve with potato pancakes. Makes 3 servings.

SideDishes

VEGETABLES

GLAZED CARROTS, APPLES, AND NUTS

For more spice flavor, use freshly grated nutmeg.

3 medium carrots, cut into
  julienne strips (1½ cups)
⅓ cup orange juice
¼ teaspoon ground cinnamon
⅛ teaspoon ground nutmeg
1 medium cooking apple, peeled
  and chopped (½ cup)
3 tablespoons cold water
1 teaspoon cornstarch
2 tablespoons chopped walnuts
  or chopped pecans

In a saucepan combine carrots, orange juice, cinnamon, and nutmeg. Bring to boiling; reduce heat. Cover and simmer 6 minutes. Add apple; cover and simmer 3 minutes more.

Stir cold water into cornstarch; stir cornstarch mixture into carrots. Cook and stir till thickened and bubbly. Cook and stir 2 minutes more. Stir in nuts. Makes 4 servings.

ZUCCHINI-CARROT STIR-FRY

Be sure to use dry sherry, not cooking sherry, which usually contains salt.

1 tablespoon cooking oil
1 teaspoon grated gingerroot
1 small clove garlic, minced
2 medium carrots, thinly sliced
  (1 cup)
2 medium zucchini, thinly sliced
  (2 cups)
3 tablespoons dry sherry

Preheat a wok or large skillet over high heat; add oil. Stir-fry gingerroot and garlic in hot oil 30 seconds. Add carrots; stir-fry 2 minutes. Add zucchini; stir-fry 2 minutes or till vegetables are crisp-tender. Stir in sherry. Makes 5 or 6 servings.

ORANGE-AND-HONEY-GLAZED SQUASH

2 medium acorn squash
  (12 to 16 ounces each)
1 cup water
2 tablespoons cold water
1 tablespoon cornstarch
½ teaspoon finely shredded
  orange peel
½ cup orange juice
2 tablespoons honey

Cut squash into quarters; discard seeds. Place, skin side down, in a 4-quart saucepan or Dutch oven. Add the 1 cup water. Bring to boiling; reduce heat. Cover and steam over medium-low heat for 15 to 20 minutes or till tender. Drain.

Meanwhile, in a small saucepan stir the 2 tablespoons cold water into the cornstarch. Stir in orange peel and orange juice. Cook and stir till thickened and bubbly. Cook and stir 2 minutes more. Stir in honey. Spoon orange juice mixture over squash. Makes 4 servings.

Pictured opposite: Glazed Carrots, Apples, and Nuts

CURRIED RICE AND VEGETABLES

Adjust the amount of curry powder to suit your taste.

½ cup chopped onion
¼ cup sliced celery
2 to 3 teaspoons curry powder
2 tablespoons cooking oil
½ cup long grain rice
1¼ cups water
1 medium zucchini, quartered lengthwise and sliced
1 medium tomato, peeled, seeded, and chopped
¼ cup coarsely chopped unsalted cashews *or* unsalted peanuts

In a 2-quart saucepan cook onion, celery, and curry powder in cooking oil till vegetables are tender but not brown. Stir in rice. Add water. Cover and bring to boiling; reduce heat. Simmer, covered, for 15 minutes. Stir in zucchini; cover and cook about 5 minutes more or till zucchini and rice are tender. Stir in tomato; heat through. Garnish with chopped cashews or peanuts. Makes 6 servings.

RATATOUILLE-TOPPED PASTA

Pictured on page 53.

¼ cup chopped onion
1 clove garlic, minced
1 tablespoon olive oil *or* cooking oil
2 medium tomatoes, peeled and chopped
1½ cups cubed peeled eggplant
1 cup sliced zucchini
½ cup chopped green pepper
2 tablespoons snipped parsley
½ teaspoon dried oregano, crushed
¼ teaspoon sugar
⅛ teaspoon pepper
4 ounces green noodles *or* regular noodles
1 tablespoon grated Parmesan cheese

In a medium saucepan cook onion and garlic in oil till tender but not brown. Add tomatoes, eggplant, zucchini, green pepper, parsley, oregano, sugar, and pepper. Bring to boiling; reduce heat. Simmer, uncovered, for 20 to 30 minutes or till excess liquid is evaporated. Stir often toward end of cooking.

Meanwhile, cook noodles according to package directions, *except* omit salt; drain well. To serve, ladle the tomato mixture over the hot cooked noodles. Sprinkle with the Parmesan cheese. Makes 4 servings.

HERBED BROCCOLI-PASTA TOSS

 4 ounces linguine *or* spaghetti
1½ cups broccoli flowerets
 ½ cup chopped onion
 ¾ cup light cream
 1 teaspoon all-purpose flour
 ¾ teaspoon dried basil, crushed
 ½ teaspoon grated lemon peel
 ¼ teaspoon dried marjoram,
    crushed
    Dash ground nutmeg

Cook linguine or spaghetti according to package directions, *except* omit the salt. Drain well. Meanwhile, cook broccoli and onion in boiling water for 5 to 8 minutes or till broccoli is crisp-tender; drain.

For sauce, in a saucepan stir together light cream, flour, basil, lemon peel, marjoram, nutmeg, and ⅛ teaspoon *pepper*. Cook and stir till thickened and bubbly. Cook and stir 1 minute more. Toss together hot pasta, vegetable mixture, and sauce. Serve at once. Makes 4 servings.

PASTA WITH PARSLEY PESTO

 8 ounces spaghetti *or* other pasta
1½ cups snipped parsley
 ⅓ cup grated Parmesan *or*
    Romano cheese
 ¼ cup walnuts
 2 teaspoons dried basil, crushed
 2 cloves garlic, quartered
 ¼ cup olive oil *or* cooking oil
    Cracked pepper

Cook pasta according to package directions, *except* omit salt; drain. Meanwhile, for pesto, in a blender container or food processor bowl combine parsley, cheese, nuts, basil, and garlic. Cover; process with several on/off turns till paste forms. Gradually add oil, processing till smooth.

Toss *half* of the pesto with the hot cooked pasta. (Refrigerate or freeze remaining pesto for another use.) Sprinkle with cracked pepper. Serve at once. Makes 8 servings.

For easy measuring, snip fresh parsley in a glass measure.

TABOULEH

Bring the garden to the table with this minty-cool salad. Purchase bulgur wheat in the supermarket or a health food shop.

1 cup bulgur wheat
1 cup warm water
1 medium tomato, peeled and chopped
½ medium cucumber, seeded and chopped
½ cup snipped parsley
2 tablespoons finely chopped green onion
1 tablespoon finely chopped fresh mint *or* 1 teaspoon dried mint, crushed
⅛ teaspoon pepper
3 tablespoons salad oil
3 tablespoons lemon juice
  Lettuce leaves
  Plain yogurt (optional)

In a bowl combine bulgur and warm water. Let stand ½ hour. Stir in tomato, cucumber, parsley, green onion, mint, and pepper. Combine oil and lemon juice. Toss with the bulgur mixture. Cover and chill. Serve in a lettuce-lined bowl with yogurt, if desired. Makes 8 servings.

VEGETABLE SALAD SHELLS

Try this new twist in pasta salads.

1 10-ounce package frozen mixed vegetables
½ cup vinegar
¼ cup salad oil
2 tablespoons sugar
2 tablespoons finely chopped green pepper
2 tablespoons finely chopped onion
½ teaspoon celery seed
½ teaspoon mustard seed
  Several dashes bottled hot pepper sauce
12 jumbo pasta shells
6 small lettuce leaves

In a saucepan cook frozen mixed vegetables according to package directions, *except* omit salt; drain. In a bowl combine vinegar, oil, sugar, green pepper, onion, celery seed, mustard seed, and hot pepper sauce; mix well. Stir in the drained cooked vegetables. Cover and chill.

Cook pasta shells according to package directions, *except* omit salt. Drain and chill. Drain vegetable mixture and spoon into shells. For each serving arrange 2 stuffed shells on a lettuce leaf. Makes 6 servings.

Pictured opposite: Vegetable Salad Shells

Side Dishes

SALADS

HOT POTATO SALAD

4 medium potatoes
½ cup sliced green onion
2 teaspoons cooking oil
2 teaspoons all-purpose flour
2 teaspoons sugar
½ teaspoon dry mustard
½ teaspoon celery seed
3 tablespoons vinegar

In a covered saucepan cook potatoes in boiling water for 25 to 30 minutes or till tender; drain well. Peel and slice potatoes. In a 10-inch skillet cook onion in oil till tender but not brown. Stir in flour, sugar, dry mustard, celery seed, and dash *pepper.* Add vinegar and ½ cup *cold water.* Cook and stir till thickened and bubbly. Cook and stir 1 minute more. Stir in the sliced, cooked potatoes. Cook about 5 minutes or till heated through, tossing lightly. Makes 4 servings.

FRUIT-AND-NUT SPAGHETTI SQUASH SALAD

1 2-pound spaghetti squash
2 medium oranges, peeled and
   sectioned
1 cup halved seedless green
   grapes
1 green onion, thinly sliced
¼ cup salad oil
2 tablespoons cider vinegar
2 teaspoons Dijon-style mustard
   or Low-Sodium Dijon-Style
   Mustard (see recipe, page 11)
1 teaspoon honey
   Lettuce leaves
¼ cup unsalted sunflower nuts *or*
   coarsely chopped unsalted
   peanuts

Cut squash into halves or quarters to fit a large saucepan or Dutch oven; discard seeds. Place squash in 1 inch of water in the saucepan. Bring to boiling; reduce heat. Cover and simmer 20 to 25 minutes or till tender. Drain; let cool. With a fork, separate pulp into strands; pile into a large bowl. Toss in oranges, grapes, and onion. Cover and chill at least 3 hours.

Meanwhile, for dressing, combine oil, vinegar, mustard, and honey. Beat smooth with a whisk or rotary beater. Cover and chill. Before serving, toss dressing with squash mixture. Serve in lettuce-lined bowl. Top with nuts. Makes 6 servings.

To separate the cooked squash into strands, use a fork to scrape out the pulp.

VEGETABLE-NUT SLAW

¾ cup broken walnuts
1 teaspoon salad oil
½ teaspoon dried dillweed
¼ teaspoon garlic powder
⅓ cup salad oil
2 tablespoons white wine vinegar
2 tablespoons lemon juice
1 teaspoon sugar
1 teaspoon Dijon-style mustard
  or Low-Sodium Dijon-Style
  Mustard (see recipe, page 11)
¼ teaspoon dried oregano, crushed
  Dash pepper
1½ cups shredded cabbage *or*
  Chinese cabbage
1½ cups shredded red cabbage
1 medium cucumber, seeded and
  cut into julienne strips
1 medium carrot, shredded
4 green onions, thinly sliced

Spread walnuts in a shallow baking pan. Sprinkle with 1 teaspoon oil, ¼ *teaspoon* of the dillweed, and the garlic powder. Toast in a 350° oven for 10 to 12 minutes, stirring once. Cool.

For dressing, in a screw-top jar combine ⅓ cup oil, the vinegar, lemon juice, sugar, mustard, oregano, pepper, and the remaining ¼ teaspoon dillweed. In a bowl combine cabbage or Chinese cabbage, red cabbage, cucumber, carrot, and onions. Shake dressing again; pour over vegetables and toss. Toss in seasoned walnuts. Makes 8 servings.

CUCUMBER-TOPPED TOSSED SALAD

If you use fresh mint, rub the inside of the salad bowl with a few mint leaves to add more flavor to the salad.

¼ cup shredded cucumber
1 tablespoon finely chopped
  green pepper
½ cup dairy sour cream
1 tablespoon milk
1 teaspoon snipped fresh mint *or*
  ¼ teaspoon dried mint,
  crushed
  Dash pepper
4 cups torn salad greens
1 cup cauliflower flowerets
½ cup thinly sliced carrot
1 medium tomato, cut into
  wedges
1 small onion, sliced and
  separated into rings

In a bowl stir together the cucumber and green pepper. Stir in the sour cream, milk, mint, and pepper. Cover and chill.

Meanwhile, in a large salad bowl toss together the greens, cauliflower, carrot, tomato, and onion. Stir sour cream mixture; if too thick, stir in a little additional milk. Spoon atop the vegetables; toss to coat. Makes 6 servings.

Side Dishes

SALADS

AVOCADO-CITRUS SALAD

Attractively arrange the lettuce and fruit on individual plates, then top with an easy orange-poppy seed dressing. An elegant salad for dinner or a luncheon!

3 white grapefruit *or* 6 oranges
2 medium avocados
6 Bibb *or* leaf lettuce leaves
1 medium red onion, thinly sliced and separated into rings
¼ cup salad oil
3 tablespoons frozen orange juice concentrate, thawed
1 tablespoon honey
1 tablespoon vinegar
½ teaspoon poppy seed

Working over a bowl to save juice, peel grapefruit or oranges. Cut each grapefruit or orange section away from the membrane and into the bowl; discard membrane. Cut avocados in half lengthwise; remove and discard seeds and peel. Slice avocados into the bowl containing the citrus sections and juice. Toss gently to coat.

Place a lettuce leaf on each of 6 individual salad plates. Arrange avocado slices and citrus sections on lettuce. Top with onion rings. For dressing, in a blender container combine salad oil, orange juice concentrate, honey, and vinegar. Cover and blend till well mixed. Stir in poppy seed. Drizzle dressing atop each salad. Makes 6 servings.

TROPICAL FRUIT SALAD

You'll have enough of the mild curry dressing for another salad. Try it on almost any fruit mixture. Or, use it on a main-dish salad of tossed greens, cubed chicken or turkey, chopped apple, raisins, and unsalted peanuts.

1 pineapple
1 cup halved seedless green grapes
1 medium apple, thinly sliced
1 medium orange, sectioned
1 medium banana, sliced
   Lettuce leaves
½ cup Sweet-Sour Curry Dressing

To make pineapple boat, use a sharp knife to cut a vertical slice from one side of the pineapple. Hollow out the pineapple, leaving ½-inch walls. If necessary, cut a slice from the base of the pineapple boat so it sits flat. Cube pineapple and reserve 1 cup (use remaining pineapple another time).

Combine reserved pineapple, the grapes, apple slices, orange sections, and banana slices. Line pineapple boat with lettuce leaves and fill with fruit mixture. Before serving, drizzle with the Sweet-Sour Curry Dressing. Makes 4 servings.

• **Sweet-Sour Curry Dressing** • In a screw-top jar combine ⅓ cup *sugar*, ¼ cup *salad oil*, ¼ cup *red wine vinegar*, 4 teaspoons *lemon juice*, ¼ teaspoon *dry mustard*, ⅛ teaspoon *curry powder*, a few dashes *bottled hot pepper sauce*, and 1 small clove *garlic*, minced. Cover and shake well to blend ingredients and dissolve sugar. Chill. Shake again just before serving. Store in the refrigerator. Makes about 1 cup.

WHITE BREAD

5¾ to 6¼ cups all-purpose flour
1 package active dry yeast
1¼ cups milk
1 cup water
2 tablespoons sugar
1 tablespoon shortening
½ teaspoon salt

In a large mixer bowl combine *2½ cups* of the flour and the yeast. In a saucepan heat milk, water, sugar, shortening, and salt just till warm (115° to 120°) and shortening is almost melted; stir constantly. Add to flour mixture. Beat with an electric mixer on low speed ½ minute, scraping the sides of the bowl. Beat on high speed 3 minutes. Stir in as much of the remaining flour as you can mix in using a spoon.

Turn out onto a lightly floured surface. Knead in enough of the remaining flour to make a moderately stiff dough that is smooth and elastic (6 to 8 minutes total). Shape into a ball. Place in a lightly greased bowl; turn once to grease surface. Cover; let rise in a warm place till double (about 1¼ hours).

Punch down; turn out onto a lightly floured surface. Divide dough in half. Cover; let rest 10 minutes. Lightly grease two 8x4x2-inch loaf pans. Shape each half of dough into a loaf. Place in pans. Cover; let rise in a warm place till nearly double (35 to 45 minutes). Bake in a 375° oven about 45 minutes or till loaf sounds hollow when tapped with your finger. Remove from the pans; cool. Makes 2 loaves (36 servings).

LOW SALT TIP

Why Yeast Breads Contain Salt

Many people are surprised to find out how much sodium is in an average slice of bread. Salt typically is present in bakery goods for several reasons. One is for flavor. Another is for controlling yeast growth so the dough doesn't rise too fast or too much. Otherwise, the bread would have an open, irregular texture.

By making your own bread, you can control the amount of salt you add. In standard bread recipes, you can use about one-fourth the amount of salt called for and still get a good-textured bread with plenty of flavor. Add sweeteners and spices to the bread and you can lower the salt even more. When breads contain salted butter or margarine, you can skip the salt entirely without sacrificing taste.

Keep in mind that when you lower the salt in bread, the dough may rise faster than usual. To keep it from rising too much, check it before the recommended rising time is up. If it has doubled (or nearly doubled for the second rising), proceed with the recipe.

HONEY-WHEAT BREAD

3 to 3½ cups all-purpose flour
1 package active dry yeast
1⅔ cups water
⅓ cup honey
¼ cup butter *or* margarine
2 cups whole wheat flour

Combine *2 cups* of the all-purpose flour and the yeast. Heat water, honey, and butter just till warm (115° to 120°), stirring constantly. Add to flour mixture. Beat with an electric mixer on low speed ½ minute, scraping sides of bowl. Beat on high speed 3 minutes. Stir in whole wheat flour and as much of the remaining all-purpose flour as you can mix in using a spoon.

On a lightly floured surface knead in enough remaining all-purpose flour to make a moderately stiff dough (6 to 8 minutes total). Shape into a ball in a lightly greased bowl; turn once. Cover; let rise in warm place till double (1 to 1½ hours).

Punch down; turn out onto a lightly floured surface. Divide in half. Cover; let rest 10 minutes. Shape into loaves; place in 2 greased 8x4x2-inch loaf pans. Cover; let rise till nearly double (30 to 45 minutes). Bake in a 375° oven for 40 to 45 minutes or till loaf sounds hollow when tapped with your finger. Cover loaves with foil the last 20 minutes to prevent overbrowning. Remove from pans; cool. Makes 2 loaves (36 servings).

HERBED FRENCH BREAD

Pictured on page 53.

5½ to 6 cups all-purpose flour
2 packages active dry yeast
1 teaspoon dried basil, crushed
½ teaspoon dried thyme, crushed
½ teaspoon dillseed
½ teaspoon salt
2 cups warm water (115° to 120°)
 Cornmeal
1 slightly beaten egg white
1 tablespoon water

Combine *2 cups* of the flour, the yeast, basil, thyme, dillseed, and salt. Add the 2 cups warm water. Beat with an electric mixer on low speed ½ minute, scraping sides of the bowl. Beat on high speed 3 minutes. Stir in as much remaining flour as you can mix in using a spoon. Turn out onto a lightly floured surface. Knead in enough remaining flour to make a stiff dough that is smooth and elastic (8 to 10 minutes total). Shape into a ball in a lightly greased bowl; turn once to grease surface. Cover; let rise in a warm place till double (1 to 1¼ hours).

Punch down; turn out onto a lightly floured surface. Divide in half. Cover; let rest 10 minutes. Roll each half into a 15x12-inch rectangle. Roll up tightly from the long side; seal well. Taper ends. Place, seam side down, on a greased baking sheet sprinkled with cornmeal. Make 3 or 4 diagonal cuts about ¼ inch deep across tops of loaves. Cover; let rise till nearly double (about 45 minutes). Carefully brush with a mixture of egg white and 1 tablespoon water. Place a pan of water on bottom shelf of oven. Bake bread in a 375° oven 40 to 45 minutes. If desired, brush again with egg white mixture after 20 minutes. Remove; cool. Makes 2 loaves (30 servings).

Pictured opposite: English Muffins (see recipe and variation, page 71), Honey-Wheat Bread

BREADS

DINNER ROLLS

4½ to 5 cups all-purpose flour
1 package active dry yeast
1 cup water
⅓ cup sugar
⅓ cup butter *or* margarine
2 eggs

Combine *2 cups* of the flour and the yeast. Heat water, sugar, and butter just till warm (115° to 120°) and butter is almost melted; stir constantly. Add to flour mixture. Add eggs. Beat with an electric mixer on low speed ½ minute, scraping sides of bowl constantly. Beat on high speed 3 minutes. Stir in as much of the remaining flour as you can mix in using a spoon.

Turn out onto a lightly floured surface. Knead in enough of the remaining flour to make a moderately stiff dough that is smooth and elastic (6 to 8 minutes total). Shape into a ball. Place in a greased bowl; turn once to grease surface. Cover; let rise in a warm place till double (about 1 hour).

Punch down; turn out onto a lightly floured surface. Divide dough in half. Cover; let rest 10 minutes. Shape each half into 12 to 15 balls; place in greased muffin cups. Cover; let rise till nearly double (about 30 minutes). Bake in a 375° oven for 12 to 15 minutes or till golden. Makes 24 to 30 servings.

• **Hamburger Buns** • Prepare dough for Dinner Rolls as above; let rise till double. Punch dough down; turn out onto a lightly floured surface. Divide into 12 portions. Cover; let rest 10 minutes. Shape each portion into an even circle, folding edges under. Press between hands to 1-inch thickness. Place on a greased baking sheet. Cover; let rise till nearly double (about 30 minutes). If desired, brush with water; sprinkle with sesame seed. Bake in a 375° oven 12 to 15 minutes or till golden. Remove from baking sheet; cool. Makes 12 servings.

YEAST BISCUITS

Refrigerate the dough several days for a stronger, sourdough flavor.

1 package active dry yeast
⅓ cup warm water (110° to 115°)
1 tablespoon sugar
2 cups all-purpose flour
½ teaspoon baking powder
½ cup shortening
⅓ cup warm milk (110° to 115°)

Soften yeast in mixture of warm water and sugar. Meanwhile, stir together flour and baking powder. Cut in shortening till mixture resembles coarse crumbs. Make a well in the center; add warm milk and yeast mixture all at once. Stir just till dough clings together. Knead gently on a lightly floured surface for 10 to 12 strokes. (At this stage, you may cover and refrigerate the dough for up to 1 week.)

Roll or pat to ½-inch thickness. Cut with a 2-inch biscuit cutter, dipping cutter in flour between cuts. Transfer to an ungreased baking sheet. Let rise for 20 to 25 minutes or till nearly double. Bake in a 450° oven 10 to 12 minutes or till golden. Serve warm. Makes 12 to 14 servings.

ENGLISH MUFFINS

*To split an English muffin, insert the tines of a fork into the side of the muffin so
they almost reach the center. Repeat around the muffin, inserting the fork right
next to the previous fork marks. Separate the halves. Pictured on page 68.*

5¼ to 5¾ cups all-purpose flour
2 packages active dry yeast
1 cup milk
1 cup water
2 tablespoons sugar
2 tablespoons shortening
¼ teaspoon salt
  Cornmeal

In a large mixer bowl stir together *2 cups* of the flour and the yeast. In a saucepan heat milk, water, sugar, shortening, and salt till warm (115° to 120°) and shortening is almost melted, stirring constantly. Add to flour mixture. Beat with an electric mixer on low speed for ½ minute, scraping the sides of the bowl constantly. Beat on high speed for 3 minutes. Stir in as much of the remaining flour as you can mix in using a spoon.

Turn out onto a lightly floured surface. Knead in enough of the remaining flour to make a moderately stiff dough that is smooth and elastic (6 to 8 minutes total). Place dough in a greased bowl; turn once to grease the surface. Cover; let rise in a warm place till double (45 minutes to 1 hour).

Punch down; cover and let rest 10 minutes. On a lightly floured surface, roll out dough to about ⅜-inch thickness. Cut with a 4-inch round cutter. Dip in cornmeal to coat both sides. Place on an ungreased baking sheet. Cover; let rise till nearly double (about 30 minutes).

Place 4 muffins on each of 3 ungreased griddles or skillets.* Cook over medium-low heat about 25 minutes or till done, turning frequently. Cool on a wire rack. Split and toast to serve. Makes 12 servings.

• **Cinnamon-Raisin English Muffins** • Prepare English Muffins as directed above, *except* add 2 teaspoons ground *cinnamon* with the yeast and stir in 1 cup *raisins* with the flour after beating dough with an electric mixer. Makes 14 servings.

*Note: If you don't have 3 skillets, work with only half of the dough at a time. Cover the remaining dough and keep refrigerated till ready to use. If desired, cut the remaining dough before refrigerating. The cut muffins will rise slightly while in the refrigerator, so they may not need all of the suggested 30 minutes to rise and nearly double.

Side Dishes

BREADS

FEATHERLIGHT PANCAKES

*Serve these soft, fluffy pancakes with your favorite topping for breakfast
or rolled up with fruit and whipped cream for dessert.*

3 eggs
½ cup milk
½ cup all-purpose flour
¼ teaspoon vanilla
2 tablespoons sugar

Separate egg yolks from whites. In a small mixer bowl beat egg yolks with an electric mixer on high speed about 3 minutes or till thick. Add milk; beat on low speed till thoroughly combined. Gradually add flour, beating on low speed till blended. Thoroughly wash beaters.

Combine egg whites and vanilla; beat with electric mixer on medium speed till soft peaks form (tips curl). Gradually add sugar, beating till stiff peaks form (tips stand straight). Stir some of the whites into the yolk mixture. By hand, fold yolk mixture into remaining whites.

For each pancake, pour ¼ cup batter onto a hot greased griddle or heavy skillet. Cook for 1 to 1½ minutes on each side or till golden. Makes about 12 pancakes (1 per serving).

CINNAMON-ORANGE POPOVERS

*The cinnamon and orange flavors are a tasty trade-off for
the salt in this classic quick bread.*

1½ teaspoons shortening
2 beaten eggs
1 cup milk
1 tablespoon cooking oil
1 cup all-purpose flour
1½ teaspoons finely shredded
   orange peel
½ teaspoon ground cinnamon

Grease *each* of six 6-ounce custard cups with ¼ *teaspoon* of the shortening. Place the custard cups in a shallow baking pan or on a baking sheet and place in the oven. Preheat the oven to 450°. Meanwhile, in a 4-cup liquid measure or mixing bowl combine beaten eggs, milk, and oil. Add flour, orange peel, and cinnamon. Beat with an electric mixer or rotary beater till mixture is smooth.

Remove the baking pan from the oven. Fill each of the hot custard cups *half* full with batter. Return the pan to the oven. Bake in the 450° oven for 10 minutes. Reduce the oven to 350°; bake 30 minutes more or till popovers are *very* firm. (If popovers brown too quickly, turn off the oven and finish baking in the cooling oven till very firm.) A few minutes before removing from the oven, prick each popover with a fork to let steam escape. Serve hot. Makes 6 servings.

Pictured opposite: Gingerbread with Lemon Sauce (see recipe, page 74)

Desserts

DESSERTS	SODIUM (mg)	Calories	Protein (g)	Carbohydrate (g)	Fat (g)	Potassium (mg)	Protein	Vitamin A	Vitamin C	Thiamine	Riboflavin	Niacin	Calcium	Iron
	Per Serving						Percent U.S. RDA Per Serving							
Berry-Honey Ice Cream (p. 78)	21	234	3	24	15	160	5	19	18	3	12	4	7	10
Burnt Almond Cream (p. 79)	36	343	4	17	29	96	7	30	1	3	9	0	9	4
Cranberry-Walnut Fruitcake (p. 75)	21	354	10	39	20	348	15	31	5	10	8	6	2	19
Fresh Fruit Pandowdy (p. 76)	29	350	3	52	16	270	4	5	8	12	7	6	4	9
Fruit Custard Tart (p. 81)	35	394	7	48	20	269	11	12	49	16	16	10	9	11
Gingerbread with Lemon Sauce (p. 74)	74	352	4	47	17	254	6	4	2	12	9	7	5	12
Hot Fruit Compote (p. 81)	10	190	2	48	0	557	3	58	13	6	7	7	4	17
Jelly Bars (p. 82)	25	103	1	11	6	35	2	2	0	3	3	2	1	2
Kiwi-Lime Ice (p. 79)	3	129	1	33	1	289	2	2	168	4	7	5	4	10
Lemon-Berry Crepes (p. 76)	57	294	5	50	9	110	7	10	9	7	10	3	6	7
Mocha Pound Cake with Java Sauce (p. 75)	48	420	6	42	27	147	9	9	0	11	11	7	6	8
Peanut Butter Fudge Brownies (p. 82)	21	98	2	12	5	44	3	1	0	2	2	3	1	2
Strawberry-Rhubarb Cream Puffs (p. 78)	27	272	5	33	14	285	7	7	77	10	11	6	7	11
Toasted Nut Macaroons (p. 82)	4	45	1	6	2	25	1	0	0	1	1	0	0	1

GINGERBREAD WITH LEMON SAUCE

Pictured on page 73.

1½ cups all-purpose flour
¾ teaspoon ground ginger
¾ teaspoon ground cinnamon
¼ teaspoon baking soda
¼ teaspoon baking powder
½ cup shortening
¼ cup packed brown sugar
2 eggs
½ cup light molasses
½ cup boiling water
⅓ cup sugar
1 tablespoon cornstarch
  Dash ground nutmeg
⅔ cup cold water
1 tablespoon butter *or* margarine
¼ teaspoon finely shredded lemon peel
1 tablespoon lemon juice

Grease and lightly flour a 9x1½-inch round or 8x8x2-inch baking pan. Stir together flour, ginger, cinnamon, baking soda, and baking powder. In large mixer bowl beat shortening with electric mixer 30 seconds. Add brown sugar. Beat till fluffy; scrape sides of bowl often, guiding mixture toward beaters.

Separate eggs; reserve egg whites and one egg yolk. Add remaining egg yolk and molasses to beaten mixture; beat 2 minutes. Add flour mixture and boiling water alternately to beaten mixture, beating after each addition. Wash beaters well. In a small mixer bowl beat reserved egg whites with electric mixer till stiff peaks form. Fold into batter; turn into prepared pan. Bake in a 350° oven for 30 to 35 minutes or till a wooden pick inserted near center comes out clean. Cool 10 minutes on a wire rack. Remove from pan; serve warm or cool.

In saucepan combine sugar, cornstarch, and nutmeg. Stir in cold water. Cook and stir till bubbly. Cook and stir 1 minute more. Beat reserved egg yolk with a fork. Stir about ½ *cup* of the hot mixture into beaten yolk; return all to saucepan. Cook and stir till bubbly; remove from heat. Stir in butter, lemon peel, and lemon juice. Serve warm over gingerbread. Serves 8.

Desserts

MOCHA POUND CAKE WITH JAVA SAUCE

Top each slice with a generous spoonful of the creamy coffee-flavored sauce.

3 eggs
1½ cups all-purpose flour
⅛ teaspoon baking soda
⅔ cup shortening
1 cup sugar
2 squares (2 ounces) unsweetened chocolate, melted and cooled
2 teaspoons instant coffee crystals
1 tablespoon hot water
½ cup dairy sour cream
1 teaspoon vanilla
Java Sauce

Bring eggs to room temperature. Grease and flour a 9x5x3-inch loaf pan. Stir together flour and baking soda. In a large mixer bowl beat shortening with electric mixer on medium speed till fluffy. Gradually add sugar, beating on medium speed about 6 minutes or till light and fluffy.

Add eggs one at a time, beating 1 minute after each; scrape the bowl frequently, guiding mixture toward the beaters. Beat in cooled, melted chocolate. In a small bowl dissolve coffee crystals in hot water; stir in sour cream and vanilla. Add flour mixture and sour cream mixture alternately to beaten mixture, beating after each addition just till combined. Turn batter into the prepared pan. Bake in a 325° oven about 1 hour or till a wooden pick inserted in center comes out clean. Cool 10 minutes on a wire rack. Remove from the pan; cool. Serve cake slices with Java Sauce. Makes 10 to 12 servings.

• **Java Sauce** • In a small bowl dissolve 1½ teaspoons instant *coffee crystals* in 2 tablespoons *hot water*. Add 1 cup dairy *sour cream*, 3 tablespoons *sugar*, and ½ teaspoon *vanilla*; stir to mix well. Cover and chill.

CRANBERRY-WALNUT FRUITCAKE

For this fruitcake, we removed the sodium-laden leavening. Also, we replaced the traditional candied fruits with fresh cranberries.

3 cups chopped walnuts
1½ cups chopped cranberries
1 cup snipped dried apricots
½ cup raisins
¾ cup all-purpose flour
¾ cup sugar
½ teaspoon ground nutmeg *or* ground mace
3 eggs
1 teaspoon vanilla
Apricot brandy *or* apricot nectar

Grease and flour an 8x4x2-inch loaf pan. In a large mixing bowl combine walnuts, cranberries, apricots, and raisins. Stir together flour, sugar, and nutmeg. Beat eggs and vanilla till foamy; stir in flour mixture just till combined. Pour over fruit mixture, stirring to mix well. Turn into the prepared pan. Cover with foil.

Bake in a 300° oven for 20 minutes. Remove foil. Bake about 1 hour 20 minutes more or till a wooden pick inserted in the center comes out clean. Cool in the pan on a wire rack; remove. Wrap in several layers of cheesecloth soaked in apricot brandy or apricot nectar. Overwrap with foil. Store in the refrigerator at least 1 week. Makes 1 fruitcake.

Desserts

FRESH FRUIT PANDOWDY

Make this homey dessert with fresh peaches, apples, or pears.

6 cups sliced, peeled peaches, apples, *or* pears
⅓ cup sugar
½ teaspoon ground cinnamon
¼ teaspoon ground nutmeg
¼ cup light molasses
1 tablespoon butter *or* margarine
1 cup all-purpose flour
½ teaspoon finely shredded lemon peel
⅓ cup shortening
1 egg yolk
2 tablespoons cold water
Light cream *or* vanilla ice cream (optional)

Place the sliced fruit in a large bowl. Combine sugar, cinnamon, and nutmeg; toss with fruit. Add molasses; stir gently. Turn fruit mixture into a 10x6x2-inch baking dish. Dot with the butter or margarine.

For pastry, combine flour and lemon peel. Cut in shortening till mixture resembles fine crumbs. Beat together egg yolk and cold water; gradually add to flour mixture, tossing to moisten. Form dough into a ball.

On a lightly floured surface roll pastry dough into an 11x7-inch rectangle; place atop fruit. Turn under and flute pastry to sides of dish. Bake in a 350° oven for 45 minutes; remove from oven. With a sharp knife, "dowdy" the crust by making several gashes through the crust and the fruit about 1 inch apart, allowing the fruit juices to seep up through crust. Return to oven; bake about 10 minutes more or till fruit is tender. Serve warm. If desired, serve with light cream or ice cream. Serves 6.

LEMON-BERRY CREPES

¾ cup milk
½ cup all-purpose flour
1 egg
1 egg yolk
1 tablespoon sugar
1 tablespoon cooking oil
½ cup sugar
2 tablespoons cornstarch
¾ cup cold water
2 beaten egg yolks
1 teaspoon finely shredded lemon peel
3 tablespoons lemon juice
1 tablespoon butter *or* margarine
½ cup blueberry *or* red raspberry preserves
1 teaspoon lemon juice

For crepes, in a blender container or food processor bowl combine milk, flour, egg, 1 egg yolk, 1 tablespoon sugar, and cooking oil. Cover; blend or process about 30 seconds or till smooth. Heat a lightly greased 6-inch skillet. Remove from heat. Spoon in *2 tablespoons* of the batter; lift and tilt skillet to spread batter. Return to heat; brown on one side only. Invert over paper toweling; remove crepe. Repeat to make 12 crepes. Grease skillet as needed.

For filling, in a heavy saucepan stir together the ½ cup sugar and the cornstarch; stir in cold water till combined. Stir in 2 beaten egg yolks and the lemon peel. Cook and stir till mixture is thickened and bubbly; cook and stir 2 minutes more. Remove from heat. Stir in 3 tablespoons lemon juice and the butter or margarine. Cover and cool.

To assemble, spread a rounded tablespoon of the filling over the unbrowned side of each crepe, leaving a ¼-inch rim around edge. Roll up jelly-roll style. Serve immediately or cover and chill. Before serving, stir together preserves and 1 teaspoon lemon juice. Top each crepe with some of the preserves mixture. Makes 6 servings (12 crepes).

Pictured opposite: Fresh Fruit Pandowdy

Desserts

STRAWBERRY-RHUBARB CREAM PUFFS

Make the cream puffs and filling ahead. At dessert time, just fill and serve.

¼ to ⅓ cup sugar
1 teaspoon finely shredded
orange peel (set aside)
4 tablespoons orange juice
8 ounces fresh *or* frozen rhubarb,
cut into 1-inch pieces (about
2 cups)
1 tablespoon cornstarch
½ cup water
¼ cup shortening
½ cup all-purpose flour
2 eggs
2 cups sliced fresh strawberries

For filling, in a medium saucepan stir together the sugar and *2 tablespoons* of the orange juice; add rhubarb. Bring to boiling; reduce heat. Cover and simmer 5 minutes or till tender. Stir the remaining 2 tablespoons orange juice into cornstarch; stir into the rhubarb mixture. Cook and stir over medium heat till thickened and bubbly. Cook and stir 2 minutes more. Chill.

For cream puffs, in a medium saucepan combine water and shortening; bring to boiling, stirring till shortening is melted. Stir in orange peel. Add flour all at once; stir vigorously. Cook and stir till the mixture forms a ball that doesn't separate. Remove from heat; cool slightly, about 5 minutes. Add eggs, one at a time, beating with a wooden spoon 1 to 2 minutes after each addition or till smooth.

Drop batter by heaping tablespoonfuls onto a greased baking sheet. Bake in a 400° oven about 30 minutes or till golden brown and puffed. Remove from oven; cool on a wire rack. Split cream puffs, removing any soft dough inside. Cool.

To serve, fold the rhubarb mixture into the sliced strawberries. Spoon strawberry-rhubarb mixture into bottom of cream puff shells and top with cream puff tops. Makes 5 servings.

BERRY-HONEY ICE CREAM

For variety, vary the berry.

1½ cups fresh *or* frozen
unsweetened boysenberries
3 egg yolks
½ teaspoon finely shredded lemon
peel
2 tablespoons lemon juice
¼ cup honey
1 cup whipping cream

Thaw boysenberries, if frozen. In a blender container or food processor bowl blend or process the berries till pureed. (*Or,* mash berries in a bowl by pressing berries against the side of the bowl with the back of a spoon.) In a small mixer bowl beat egg yolks with electric mixer on high speed about 5 minutes or till thick and lemon colored. Beat in lemon peel and lemon juice. Beat in the pureed berries and honey.

Beat whipping cream till soft peaks form; fold into berry mixture. Turn mixture into an 8x8x2-inch baking pan. Cover; freeze several hours or till nearly solid. Break up frozen mixture in chilled mixer bowl. Beat with electric mixer till smooth. Return to pan. Cover; freeze. Makes 6 (½-cup) servings.

KIWI-LIME ICE

Easy, delicious, and unusual.

2 **kiwifruit, peeled and mashed**
¼ **cup water**
2 **tablespoons honey**
4 **teaspoons lime juice**

In a small bowl combine kiwifruit, water, honey, and lime juice. Cover and freeze till firm. Before serving, let mixture stand at room temperature for 5 minutes. Scrape across top with a spoon and pile into dessert dishes. Makes 2 servings.

BURNT ALMOND CREAM

5 **beaten egg yolks**
2 **cups whipping cream**
¼ **cup sugar**
¼ **teaspoon almond extract**
3 **tablespoons sugar**

Beat together yolks, cream, ¼ cup sugar, and extract. Place an 8-inch quiche dish or 8x1½-inch round baking dish in a 13x9x2-inch baking pan. Pour mixture into quiche dish. Pour boiling water into larger pan to depth of ½ inch. Bake in 325° oven 40 to 45 minutes or till a knife inserted near center comes out clean. Remove quiche dish; cool. Chill at least 3 hours.

Return quiche dish to the larger pan. Fill the larger pan with ice cubes so they surround the quiche dish. Sprinkle the 3 tablespoons sugar evenly over custard. Broil 3 inches from heat for 5 or 6 minutes or till sugar is golden. Serve at once or chill. To serve, crack the sugary top with the back of a spoon. Spoon out of the dish. Makes 6 servings.

To keep custard from overcooking during broiling, place it in a larger pan and surround with ice cubes. Sprinkle on sugar and broil till golden.

FRUIT CUSTARD TART

If fresh strawberries are unavailable, use frozen ones.

2 cups all-purpose flour
2 teaspoons finely shredded
   orange peel
⅔ cup shortening
6 to 7 tablespoons orange juice
1 envelope unflavored gelatin
¼ cup sugar
2 cups milk
6 beaten egg yolks
1 teaspoon vanilla
½ cup red currant jelly
⅓ cup orange juice
1 tablespoon cornstarch
2½ cups halved fresh strawberries
1 8-ounce can peach slices
   (juice pack), drained
1 small banana, sliced

In a mixing bowl stir together flour and orange peel. Cut in shortening till mixture resembles coarse crumbs. Sprinkle *1 tablespoon* of the orange juice over part of the mixture; gently toss with a fork. Push to the side of the bowl. Repeat with the rest of the 6 to 7 tablespoons orange juice till all is moistened. Form dough into a ball. On a lightly floured surface roll dough into a 14-inch circle. Ease into a 12-inch pizza pan. Trim and flute edge high; prick pastry. Bake in a 400° oven for 12 to 15 minutes or till golden; cool.

For custard, in a saucepan combine gelatin and sugar. Stir in milk; bring mixture to boiling, stirring constantly. Gradually stir about *1 cup* of the hot mixture into the beaten egg yolks. Return mixture to saucepan; cook and stir 2 minutes more. Stir in vanilla. Chill by setting in a container of ice water, stirring to the consistency of unbeaten egg whites (partially set). Pour custard over crust. Chill about 1 hour or till set.

For glaze, in a small saucepan heat jelly over low heat till melted. Stir ⅓ cup orange juice into the cornstarch; stir into melted jelly. Cook and stir till thickened and bubbly; cook and stir 2 minutes more. Cool slightly. Meanwhile, arrange strawberry halves, peach slices, and banana slices atop custard. Spoon *half* of the glaze over the arranged fruit. Chill 20 minutes. Repeat with remaining glaze. Cover and chill. Cut into wedges to serve. Makes about 10 servings.

HOT FRUIT COMPOTE

Use the juice from the juice-pack pineapple for cooking the fruit.
The recipe needs no additional sweetening.

1 15¼-ounce can pineapple
   chunks (juice pack)
1 12-ounce package pitted, dried
   prunes
1 6-ounce package dried apricots
1½ cups water
¼ cup dry white wine

In a 1½-quart casserole combine the *undrained* pineapple chunks, prunes, and apricots. Combine water and wine; pour over fruit. Cover and bake in a 350° oven about 1 hour or till fruit is tender. Serve warm. Makes 8 servings.

Pictured opposite: Fruit Custard Tart

Desserts

PEANUT BUTTER FUDGE BROWNIES

¼ cup shortening
¼ cup chunk-style peanut butter
2 squares (2 ounces) unsweetened chocolate
1 cup sugar
2 eggs
1 teaspoon vanilla
¾ cup all-purpose flour

Grease an 8x8x2-inch baking pan. In a medium saucepan melt shortening, peanut butter, and chocolate, stirring constantly. Remove from heat; stir in sugar. Add eggs and vanilla. Beat *lightly* just till combined (don't overbeat or brownies will rise too high, then fall). Stir in the flour. Spread batter in the prepared pan. Bake in a 350° oven about 25 minutes or till a slight imprint remains when touched lightly. Cool. Cut into bars. Makes 25 servings.

JELLY BARS

½ cup sugar
¼ cup butter *or* margarine
¼ cup shortening
1 egg yolk
½ cup ground almonds
½ teaspoon finely shredded lemon peel
¾ cup all-purpose flour
¼ teaspoon ground cinnamon
⅓ cup jelly *or* jam
2 tablespoons finely chopped almonds

In a small mixer bowl beat together sugar, butter or margarine, and shortening till fluffy. Beat in egg yolk. Stir in the ½ cup ground almonds and the lemon peel. Stir together flour and cinnamon. Stir into beaten mixture. With floured fingers, pat about *two-thirds* of the dough into the bottom of an ungreased 8x8x2-inch baking pan. Bake in a 350° oven for 10 minutes. Drop jelly by spoonfuls evenly atop. If necessary, spread gently. Dot with remaining dough. Sprinkle with the 2 tablespoons chopped almonds. Bake 20 to 25 minutes more or till top is golden. Cool. Cut into bars. Makes 24 servings.

TOASTED NUT MACAROONS

¾ cup chopped unsalted cashews, almonds, *or* peanuts
2 egg whites
½ teaspoon vanilla
⅔ cup sugar
¾ cup flaked coconut

Spread nuts evenly in a shallow baking pan. Toast in a 350° oven 10 minutes or till brown, stirring occasionally. Set aside.

Grease a cookie sheet. In a mixer bowl combine egg whites and vanilla; beat with an electric mixer till soft peaks form. Gradually add sugar, beating till stiff peaks form. Fold in coconut and nuts. Drop from a teaspoon 1½ inches apart onto the greased cookie sheet. Bake in a 325° oven about 20 minutes or till light brown on bottom. Cool. Makes 30 servings.

Pictured opposite: Fresh Vegetable Pâté (see recipe, page 84), Country Oat Snackers (see recipe, page 85), Party Nut Mix (see recipe, page 85), and Spicy Tomato-Cucumber Sipper (see recipe, page 87)

Snacks and Beverages

SNACKS AND BEVERAGES	SODIUM (mg)	Calories	Protein (g)	Carbohydrate (g)	Fat (g)	Potassium (mg)	Protein	Vitamin A	Vitamin C	Thiamine	Riboflavin	Niacin	Calcium	Iron
	Per Serving						Percent U.S. RDA Per Serving							
Country Oat Snackers (p. 85)	0	44	1	4	3	25	2	0	0	3	1	1	0	2
Cranberry-Banana Nog (p. 87)	30	77	3	13	2	142	4	3	15	3	6	1	5	3
Fresh Fruit Fritters (p. 86)	2	33	0	6	1	28	1	1	2	1	1	1	0	1
Fresh Vegetable Pâté (p. 84)	16	21	1	1	2	45	1	8	12	1	2	0	1	1
Honey-Crunch Granola (p. 86)	5	139	3	17	7	154	5	0	1	10	4	3	2	6
Party Nut Mix (p. 85)	18	195	6	15	13	147	9	3	0	5	3	15	3	4
Peanut-Raisin Spread (p. 85)	1	57	2	4	4	86	3	0	6	2	1	7	1	1
Spicy Tomato-Cucumber Sipper (p. 87)	12	27	1	6	0	283	2	19	31	4	2	5	1	6
Tropical Slush (p. 87)	2	139	1	36	0	265	1	2	34	4	3	3	1	3

FRESH VEGETABLE PÂTÉ

Serve this refreshing pâté with purchased low-sodium crackers, matzo wafers, or the Country Oat Snackers on the next page. Both the pâté and homemade crackers are pictured on page 83.

1 envelope unflavored gelatin
⅓ cup cold water
⅔ cup plain yogurt
¼ teaspoon dried dillweed
1½ cups broccoli flowerets
1 medium carrot, sliced
1 stalk celery, sliced (½ cup)
1 slice onion
2 3-ounce packages cream cheese, cut into cubes and softened
Shredded zucchini

In a small saucepan soften gelatin in cold water; heat and stir over low heat till gelatin is dissolved. Remove from heat.

In a blender container or food processor bowl combine the yogurt, dillweed, and gelatin mixture; add broccoli, carrot, celery, and onion. Cover; blend or process till vegetables are coarsely chopped. Add cream cheese; blend till smooth. Turn into a lightly greased 3-cup mold or bowl. Cover and refrigerate for 6 hours or overnight.

To serve, unmold pâté onto a bed of shredded zucchini. Makes about 2½ cups or 40 (1-tablespoon) servings.

PEANUT-RAISIN SPREAD

Great on apple wedges, banana slices, carrot sticks, or low-sodium crackers.

2 cups unsalted peanuts
1 tablespoon honey *or* molasses
½ teaspoon ground cinnamon
1 cup orange juice
½ cup raisins

Place peanuts in a food processor bowl. Cover; process with metal blade for 3 to 5 minutes or till a paste forms, scraping the sides of the bowl occasionally. (*Or,* in a blender container cover and blend *one-third* of the peanuts at a time, stopping the blender and scraping the sides frequently.) Mix in honey and cinnamon. With the machine running, pour in orange juice; process till smooth. Add raisins; process just till mixed in. Makes 2¼ cups or 36 (1-tablespoon) servings.

COUNTRY OAT SNACKERS

*These are great to have around when the "munchies" strike.
Pictured on page 83.*

1½ cups quick-cooking
    or regular rolled oats
½ cup all-purpose flour
⅓ cup toasted wheat germ
2 tablespoons sesame seed
1 tablespoon sugar
⅛ teaspoon onion powder
⅓ cup shortening
⅓ cup water

Place oats in blender container or food processor bowl. Cover; blend or process about 1 minute or till evenly ground. In a mixing bowl combine oats, flour, wheat germ, sesame seed, sugar, and onion powder. Cut in shortening till mixture resembles coarse crumbs. Gradually add water, mixing till dry ingredients are moistened. Shape into a 9-inch log. Cut into ¼-inch slices. Place on ungreased baking sheet. Flatten with tines of a fork or a meat mallet till very thin; dip utensil in flour as needed to prevent sticking. Bake in a 375° oven 18 to 20 minutes or till edges are brown. Remove; cool. Makes 36.

PARTY NUT MIX

This mix looks salty, but actually has very little salt. Pictured on page 83.

4 cups bite-size shredded
    wheat biscuits
2 cups unsalted peanuts
½ cup cooking oil
⅛ teaspoon bottled hot
    pepper sauce
¼ cup grated Parmesan cheese
2 teaspoons chili powder
½ teaspoon garlic powder
4 cups unsalted pretzels

In a large roasting pan combine shredded wheat biscuits and peanuts. Stir together the cooking oil and hot pepper sauce; drizzle over cereal mixture, tossing to coat evenly. Stir together Parmesan cheese, chili powder, and garlic powder; toss with cereal mixture. Bake in a 300° oven for 20 minutes, stirring after 10 minutes. Stir in the pretzels. Bake 10 minutes more. Makes about 10 cups or 20 (½-cup) servings.

HONEY-CRUNCH GRANOLA

*If you like, substitute snipped dried apricots or chopped mixed dried fruit
for all or part of the raisins.*

3 cups regular *or* quick-cooking
  rolled oats
½ cup coconut
½ cup coarsely chopped almonds
½ cup sesame seed
½ cup unsalted sunflower nuts
½ cup toasted wheat germ
½ cup honey
¼ cup cooking oil
½ teaspoon ground cinnamon
½ teaspoon vanilla
1 cup raisins

In a 13x9x2-inch baking pan stir together the oats, coconut, almonds, sesame seed, sunflower nuts, and wheat germ. Combine honey, oil, cinnamon, and vanilla; stir into oat mixture till well coated. Spread evenly in the pan. Bake in a 350° oven 25 to 30 minutes or till light brown, stirring every 10 minutes. Stir in raisins; cool. Makes about 7 cups or 28 (¼-cup) servings.

FRESH FRUIT FRITTERS

*These make great snacks any time of day. They're also ideal as a brunch
appetizer or, at the other end of the meal, a light dessert.*

Fresh apples, strawberries,
  pears, bananas, *or* pineapple
1 beaten egg
⅓ cup cornstarch
⅓ cup all-purpose flour
2 tablespoons sugar
2 tablespoons orange juice
1 teaspoon vanilla
  Cooking oil for deep-fat frying
  Sifted powdered sugar
  Vanilla yogurt (optional)

If necessary, peel and core the fruit; cut into 1- to 1½-inch pieces. In a bowl beat together the egg, cornstarch, flour, sugar, orange juice, and vanilla till smooth. In a saucepan or wok pour in oil to a depth of 2 inches. Heat oil to 365°. Dip fruit pieces individually into batter, swirling to coat. Drain off excess batter. Fry fruit pieces, a few at a time, in hot oil for 2 to 3 minutes or till golden brown. Drain on paper toweling. Sprinkle with powdered sugar. If desired, serve with vanilla yogurt for dipping. Makes 32 servings (1 per serving).

SPICY TOMATO-CUCUMBER SIPPER

Ease up on the hot pepper sauce for a less spicy drink. Pictured on page 83.

½ medium cucumber
2 cups cold water
1 6-ounce can tomato paste
3 tablespoons lemon juice
½ teaspoon onion powder
¼ teaspoon bottled hot pepper sauce

Peel the cucumber; halve lengthwise and remove seeds. Cut cucumber into pieces. In a blender container or food processor bowl combine cucumber, *1 cup* of the water, the tomato paste, lemon juice, onion powder, and hot pepper sauce. Cover and blend or process till smooth. Stir in remaining 1 cup water. Chill. If desired, garnish each with a strip of cucumber peel, a cucumber stick, or green onion. Makes 6 (4-ounce) servings.

TROPICAL SLUSH

Mix the fruit juice base and freeze. When you need a refresher, just add the fizz.

1½ cups unsweetened pineapple juice
1 6-ounce can frozen lemonade concentrate
2 ripe medium bananas, cut up
1½ cups mineral water
Pineapple slices (optional)

In a blender container combine pineapple juice, lemonade concentrate, and bananas. Cover and blend till smooth. Pour into an 8x4x2-inch loaf pan. Cover; freeze till firm.

Before serving, thaw for 30 minutes. Scrape across surface with a spoon. Spoon about *½ cup* of the scraped slush mixture into each glass. Pour about *¼ cup* mineral water over slush in each glass. Stir gently. Garnish each serving with a pineapple slice, if desired. Makes 6 (6-ounce) servings.

CRANBERRY-BANANA NOG

Wake up or wind down with this smooth nog.

1 medium banana, cut up
1 8-ounce carton plain yogurt
1 cup cranberry juice cocktail
1 egg
¼ teaspoon vanilla
2 *or* 3 ice cubes

In a blender container combine the banana pieces, yogurt, cranberry juice cocktail, egg, and vanilla. Cover and blend till smooth and frothy. With blender running, add ice cubes, one at a time through hole in lid or with lid ajar, blending till smooth after each addition. Pour into glasses. Serve immediately. Makes 6 (4-ounce) servings.

A-B   mg Sodium

APPLE BUTTER; 1 tablespoon 0
APPLES
fresh; 1 medium...2
juice, canned; 1 cup 2
APPLESAUCE, canned; ½ cup 3
APRICOTS
canned, in syrup; ½ cup 1
dried, uncooked; ½ cup 17
fresh; 3 medium...1
nectar, canned; 1 cup...0
ASPARAGUS
canned, cut, drained; ½ cup 278
cooked without salt; 4 medium spears 1
frozen, cooked without salt; 4 medium spears......1
AVOCADO, peeled; ½ avocado...........................5
BACON
bits, imitation; 1 teaspoon...................................40
Canadian-style, cooked; 1 slice (1 ounce) 537
crisp strips, medium thickness; 2.......................153
BAKING POWDER; 1 teaspoon.....................329
BAKING SODA; 1 teaspoon.............................821
BANANA; 1 medium 1
BARBECUE SAUCE, bottled; ¼ cup..............510
BEANS
baked, with tomato sauce and pork, canned;
   ½ cup...591
green snap, canned, drained; ½ cup..................160
green snap, cooked without salt; ½ cup 3
green snap, frozen, cooked without salt; ½ cup...1
lima, canned, drained; ½ cup 200
lima, cooked without salt; ½ cup..........................2
lima, frozen, cooked without salt; ½ cup 86
BEAN SPROUTS, fresh; ½ cup...........................3
BEEF
beef for stew, lean only, cooked cubes; ½ cup...37
corned, canned; 3 ounces 893
corned, cooked; 3 ounces 802
ground beef, cooked, 10% fat; 3 ounces 57
ground beef, cooked, 21% fat; 3 ounces 49
rib roast, cooked, lean only; 3 ounces..................41
round steak, cooked, lean only; 3 ounces...........65
sirloin steak, cooked, lean only; 3 ounces 67
BEEF LIVER, fried; 3 ounces 156
BEETS
canned, sliced, drained; ½ cup 200
cooked without salt, sliced; ½ cup.......................37
BEVERAGES, alcoholic
beer; 12 ounces 25
dessert wine; 1 ounce 1
gin, rum, vodka, *or* whiskey; 1 ounce...................0
table wine; 1 ounce...1

BEVERAGES, nonalcoholic
club soda; 8 ounces...39
cocoa mix, water added; 8 ounces 232
coffee; 8 ounces 2
cola; 8 ounces..16
ginger ale; 8 ounces 13
root beer; 8 ounces 24
tea; 8 ounces 1
BISCUIT, made from mix;
1 (2-inch diameter)...272
BLACKBERRIES, fresh *or* frozen; ½ cup.............1
BLUEBERRIES, fresh *or* frozen; ½ cup.................1
BOUILLON
cube; 1...960
instant granules; 1 teaspoon.............................480
BREAD
Boston brown; 1 slice (3¼x½ inches)..............113
corn bread; 1 piece (2½x2½x1½ inches) 263
crumbs, dry; ¼ cup...184
crumbs, soft; ¼ cup...57
cubes; 1 cup..152
French; 1 slice (2½x2x½ inches).......................87
Italian; 1 slice (4½x3¼x¾ inches)....................176
pumpernickel; 1 slice...182
raisin; 1 slice 91
rye; 1 slice 139
stuffing, prepared from mix; ½ cup..................504
white; 1 slice...142
whole wheat; 1 slice..148
BROCCOLI
cooked without salt; 2 medium spears 8
frozen, chopped, cooked without salt; ½ cup.....28
BRUSSELS SPROUTS
cooked without salt; ½ cup..................................8
frozen, cooked without salt; ½ cup....................11
BUTTER
regular; 1 tablespoon 140
unsalted; 1 tablespoon..2
BUTTERMILK; 1 cup 319

C   mg Sodium

CABBAGE
common varieties, raw, shredded; 1 cup 14
red, raw, shredded; 1 cup....................................18
CAKE, baked from home recipes
angel, no icing; $\frac{1}{12}$ cake 170
chocolate, 2 layers, chocolate icing;
   2-inch wedge 233
fruitcake; 1 slice (2x1½x½ inches) 48
gingerbread; 1 piece (3x3x2 inches)..................277

CAKE *(continued)*
pound; 1 slice (3½x3x¾ inches) 78
sponge, no icing; 1/12 cake....................................73
white, uncooked white icing; 1/12 cake 243
yellow, chocolate icing; 1/12 cake........................208

CANDY
caramels; 1 ounce (3 medium) 64
chocolate fudge; 1 piece (1 cubic inch)..............40
hard; 1 ounce 9
jelly beans; 1 ounce (about 10) 3
marshmallows; ½ cup tiny *or* 4 regular 11
peanut brittle; 1 ounce 145
taffy; 1 ounce...88

CANTALOUPE; ¼ medium
(5-inch diameter)..17

CARROTS
canned, sliced, drained; ½ cup 183
cooked without salt, sliced; ½ cup.....................26
raw; 1 medium...34

CATSUP; 1 tablespoon 156

CAULIFLOWER
cooked without salt; ½ cup 6
frozen, cooked without salt; ½ cup......................9
raw, whole flowerets; 1 cup................................13

CELERY
celery salt; 1 teaspoon 1,430
raw; 1 stalk...50

CEREAL, cooked without salt
oatmeal; ½ cup..0
wheat, rolled; ½ cup 0

CEREAL, ready-to-eat
bite-size shredded wheat biscuits; ½ cup 1
bran flakes; ½ cup 104
cornflakes; ½ cup..125
granola; ¼ cup..61
rice, crisp cereal; ½ cup......................................159
rice, puffed; ½ cup...0
wheat flakes; ½ cup..155
wheat, puffed; ½ cup..1
wheat, puffed, with sugar and salt; ½ cup 28
whole bran cereal; 1/3 cup....................................160

CHEESE
American, process; 1 ounce................................322
blue; 1 ounce...396
brick; 1 ounce 159
Brie; 1 ounce 178
Camembert; 1 ounce 239
cheddar; 1 ounce..198
cottage, cream-style; ½ cup................................240
cottage, dry; ½ cup 210
cream cheese; 1 ounce 71

CHEESE *(continued)*
Edam; 1 ounce 274
farmer; 1 ounce..82
feta; 1 ounce 316
Monterey Jack; 1 ounce......................................152
mozzarella; 1 ounce 132
Neufchâtel; 1 ounce..113
Parmesan, grated; 1 tablespoon 44
provolone; 1 ounce...248
ricotta, part skim milk; ½ cup 154
Roquefort; 1 ounce..513
spread, American; 1 ounce 461
Swiss (natural); 1 ounce 201

CHERRIES
canned (heavy syrup), sweet, pitted; ½ cup 2
fresh, sweet, whole; 10 cherries 1

CHICKEN
dark meat, skinned, roasted; 4 ounces..............100
light meat, skinned, roasted; 4 ounces................75

CHICKEN LIVERS, cooked, chopped; 1 cup 85

CHILI POWDER; 1 teaspoon............................31

CHOCOLATE
semisweet; 1 ounce..1
sweet, plain; 1 ounce 9
syrup, fudge-type; 1 tablespoon 17
syrup, thin-type; 1 tablespoon............................10
unsweetened; 1 ounce 1

CLAMS, raw
hard; 3 ounces...174
soft; 3 ounces...30

COCOA POWDER, unsweetened
1 tablespoon...0

COCONUT, fresh, shredded; ½ cup 9

COOKIES
chocolate chip; 1 (2¼-inch diameter)..................42
cream sandwich, chocolate; 1..............................48
fig bar; 1...35
gingersnap; 1 (2-inch diameter) 40
macaroon; 1 (2¾-inch diameter) 7
sugar; 1 (2¼-inch diameter) 25
vanilla wafer; 3 (1⅜-inch diameter)....................25

CORN
canned, cream-style; ½ cup.................................302
canned, vacuum packed,
    whole kernel; ½ cup 195
cooked without salt; ½ cup....................................0
frozen, cooked without salt; ½ cup.......................1

CORN CHIPS; 1 ounce 202
CORNMEAL; 1 cup..1
CORNSTARCH; 1 tablespoon...........................0
CORN SYRUP; 1 tablespoon 14

CRAB MEAT
canned, drained; 3 ounces 425
cooked without salt; 3 ounces...........................314
CRACKERS
butter, rectangular; 1 42
cheese, round; 1...36
graham; 2 squares...95
oyster; 10 83
rye wafer, crisp; 2 (3½x1⅞ inches)..................115
saltine; 2 (2-inch squares) 62
CRANBERRIES
cranberry juice cocktail; 1 cup 3
cranberry-orange relish; ¼ cup 1
cranberry sauce; ½ cup....................................2
CREAM
light; 1 tablespoon 7
whipping; 1 tablespoon.....................................5
CUCUMBER; 6 large slices (1 ounce) 2

D-G   mg Sodium

DATES, fresh *or* dried, pitted; 10 1
DOUGHNUTS
cake-type, plain; 1 medium 210
yeast-type; 1 medium 99
EGG
white; 1 large 48
whole; 1 large 61
yolk; 1 large 9
EGGPLANT
cooked without salt, diced; ½ cup 1
FIGS, dried; 1 large 2
FISH
cod, broiled with butter; 3 ounces 93
flounder, baked with butter; 3 ounces 201
haddock, fried; 3 ounces 150
halibut, broiled with butter; 3 ounces 114
herring, smoked; 3 ounces.............................5,234
ocean perch, fried; 3 ounces............................129
salmon, broiled with butter; 3 ounces.................99
salmon, canned, pink; 3 ounces 443
sardines, canned, in oil, drained; 3 ounces 699
tuna, canned, in oil; 3 ounces...........................303
tuna, canned, in water; 3 ounces 288
FLOUR, wheat
all-purpose; 1 cup..3
whole wheat; 1 cup 4
FRANKFURTER, cooked; 1 medium...............627
FRUIT COCKTAIL, canned, in syrup; ½ cup......7

GARLIC
garlic powder; 1 teaspoon 1
garlic salt; 1 teaspoon 1,850
1 clove...1
GELATIN, dry, unflavored; 1 envelope...............0
GELATIN DESSERT, ready-to-serve; ½ cup....61
GOOSE, cooked; 3 ounces...............................105
GRAPEFRUIT
canned sections, in syrup; ½ cup 2
fresh; ½ medium...1
juice, canned, unsweetened; 1 cup......................2
GRAPES
concord, fresh; ½ cup 2
green, fresh, seedless; ½ cup 3
juice, canned; 1 cup...5

H-O   mg Sodium

HAM, fully cooked, lean only; 3 ounces...........770
HONEY; 1 tablespoon 1
HONEYDEW MELON;
¼ medium (6½-inch diameter)......................45
HORSERADISH, prepared; 1 tablespoon 198
HOT PEPPER SAUCE; 1 teaspoon....................24
ICE CREAM, vanilla
ice milk; 1 cup 89
regular; 1 cup 84
soft-serve; 1 cup 109
JAM; 1 tablespoon..2
JELLY; 1 tablespoon 3
KITCHEN BOUQUET; 1 teaspoon....................12
LAMB, cooked
loin chop, lean only; 3 ounces............................60
rib chop, lean only; 3 ounces 58
roast leg, lean only; 3 ounces 60
LARD; 1 tablespoon...0
LEMONADE
frozen, sweetened, reconstituted; 1 cup 1
LEMON JUICE; 1 tablespoon.............................0
LENTILS, cooked without salt; ½ cup 2
LETTUCE
Boston; ¼ medium head...................................4
iceberg; ¼ compact medium head.....................12
iceberg; 1 leaf (5x4½ inches) 2
LIMEADE
frozen, sweetened, reconstituted; 1 cup 0
LIME JUICE; 1 tablespoon 0
LOBSTER, cooked without salt; ½ cup............153
MACARONI, cooked without salt; ½ cup...........1
MAPLE SYRUP; 1 tablespoon.............................2

MARGARINE
regular; 1 tablespoon 140
unsalted; 1 tablespoon...............................1
MEAT TENDERIZER; 1 teaspoon................1,760
MILK
condensed, sweetened, undiluted; 1 cup 343
dried nonfat, instant, reconstituted; 1 cup 120
evaporated, undiluted; 1 cup 297
low-fat (2%); 1 cup...150
skim; 1 cup...127
whole; 1 cup 122
MOLASSES, light; 1 tablespoon 3
MUFFIN, baked from home recipes
blueberry; 1..253
bran; 1...179
English; 1 251
plain; 1 176
MUSHROOMS
canned, sliced; 2 ounces 242
fresh, sliced; 1 cup..11
MUSTARD
Dijon-style; 1 teaspoon.....................................65
dry; 1 teaspoon 0
prepared; 1 teaspoon 63
NECTARINE, fresh; 1 (2½-inch diameter) 8
NOODLES, cooked without salt; ½ cup.............2
NUTS
almonds, roasted, salted; 1 ounce (about 22) 56
almonds, shelled, chopped; ¼ cup 1
Brazil nuts; 3...0
cashews, dry roasted, salted; ¼ cup 300
cashews, roasted, unsalted; ¼ cup 7
peanuts, dry roasted, salted; ¼ cup...................247
peanuts, roasted, unsalted; ¼ cup.........................2
pecans, chopped; ¼ cup..0
walnuts, chopped; ¼ cup.......................................1
OIL, corn, olive, or soybean; 1 tablespoon 0
OKRA
cooked without salt; 10 pods (3x⅝ inches) 2
frozen, cut, cooked without salt; ½ cup................2
OLIVES
green; 4 medium..323
ripe; 4 medium..128
ONIONS
cooked without salt, sliced; ½ cup 8
green, with tops; 2 medium 2
onion powder; 1 teaspoon.....................................1
onion salt; 1 teaspoon....................................1,620
ORANGES
fresh; 1 medium..1
juice, frozen concentrate, reconstituted; 1 cup 2
OYSTERS, raw; ½ cup (6 to 10 medium) 88

P-S	mg Sodium

PANCAKES, baked from mix;
1 (4-inch diameter)...152
PARSLEY, snipped; 1 tablespoon......................2
PARSNIPS, cooked without salt, diced; ½ cup ...6
PEACHES
canned, in syrup; 1 half and
  2 tablespoons syrup..2
fresh; 1 medium..1
PEANUT BUTTER; 1 tablespoon 97
PEARS
canned, in syrup; 1 half and 2 tablespoons
  syrup 1
fresh; 1 medium..3
PEAS
canned, drained; ½ cup.....................................200
frozen, cooked without salt; ½ cup....................92
PEPPERS, green, sweet, chopped; ½ cup 10
PICKLE RELISH, sweet; 1 tablespoon.............107
PICKLES
dill; 1 large (4x1¾ inches)..............................1,928
sweet; 1 medium (2¾x¾ inches).....................128
PIE; ⅛ of a 9-inch pie
apple...355
blueberry...316
cherry..359
custard...327
lemon meringue..296
pumpkin..244
PIE SHELL, baked; one 9-inch.......................138
PINEAPPLE
canned, in syrup; ½ cup 2
fresh, diced; ½ cup...1
juice, canned, unsweetened; 1 cup........................3
PLUMS
canned, in syrup; ½ cup 2
fresh; 1 (2-inch diameter).....................................1
POPCORN, plain, popped; 1 cup......................0
PORK, cooked
chop, loin center cut, lean only; 3 ounces 61
picnic shoulder, fresh, lean only; 3 ounces..........43
POTATO CHIPS; 10 medium...........................200
POTATOES
baked; 1 medium...6
French-fried, frozen, oven heated; 10 medium 2
sweet, baked; 1 medium......................................14
sweet, canned, vacuum packed; ½ cup...............48
PRETZELS; 10 small sticks..............................101
PRUNE JUICE, canned; 1 cup 5
PRUNES, dried
cooked, unsweetened; ½ cup 5
uncooked, pitted; ½ cup.......................................7

PUMPKIN, canned; 1 cup 5
RADISHES, raw; 5 medium 4
RAISINS; 1 cup 39
RASPBERRIES, fresh, black or red; ½ cup 1
RHUBARB, cooked, sweetened; ½ cup 3
RICE
brown, cooked without salt; ½ cup 0
white, cooked without salt; ½ cup 0
ROLL
cloverleaf; 1 (2½-inch diameter) 142
hamburger or frankfurter bun; 1 202
hard; 1 medium 313
sweet; 1 medium 238
SALAD DRESSING
blue cheese; 1 tablespoon 164
French; 1 tablespoon 219
Italian; 1 tablespoon 314
mayonnaise; 1 tablespoon 84
mayonnaise-type; 1 tablespoon 88
Russian; 1 tablespoon 130
Thousand Island; 1 tablespoon 112
SALT; 1 teaspoon 2,132
SAUERKRAUT, canned; ½ cup 878
SAUSAGES AND LUNCHEON MEAT
bologna; 1 slice 224
bratwurst, cooked; 1 ounce 158
deviled ham; 1 ounce 253
liver cheese; 1 slice 245
pepperoni; 1 ounce 571
pork sausage, cooked; 1 link 168
salami, cooked; 1 slice 234
Thüringer cervelat; 1 slice 320
SCALLOPS, cooked without salt; 3 ounces 225
SEASONED SALT; 1 teaspoon 1,230
SHERBET, orange; ½ cup 10
SHORTENING; 1 tablespoon 0
SHRIMP
canned; 3 ounces 1,955
French-fried; 3 ounces 159
SOUP, condensed, canned, diluted with water unless specified otherwise
beef bouillon, broth, or consommé; 1 cup 782
beef noodle; 1 cup 917
chicken broth; 1 cup 722
chicken noodle; 1 cup 979
clam chowder, Manhattan-style; 1 cup 938
cream of celery, diluted with milk; 1 cup 1,039
cream of mushroom, diluted with milk; 1 cup 1,039

SOUP (continued)
split pea; 1 cup 941
tomato; 1 cup 970
tomato, diluted with milk; 1 cup 1,055
vegetable with beef broth; 1 cup 845
SOUR CREAM, dairy; 1 cup 123
SOY SAUCE; 1 teaspoon 440
SPAGHETTI, cooked without salt; ½ cup 0
SPAGHETTI SAUCE, meatless; ½ cup 770
SPINACH
canned, drained; ½ cup 242
fresh, torn; 1 cup 39
frozen, chopped, cooked without salt; ½ cup 54
SQUASH
summer, cooked without salt, diced; ½ cup 1
winter, baked, mashed; ½ cup 1
STRAWBERRIES
fresh, whole; 1 cup 1
frozen, sweetened, whole; 1 cup 3
SUGAR
brown; 1 tablespoon 4
granulated; 1 tablespoon 0
powdered; 1 tablespoon 0

T-Z mg Sodium

TARTAR SAUCE; 1 tablespoon 99
TOFU (soybean curd); 1 pound 36
TOMATOES
canned; ½ cup 157
fresh; 1 medium 4
juice, canned; 1 cup 486
paste, canned; 6 ounces 65
sauce, canned; 8 ounces 1,521
TURKEY, roasted; 3 slices (3 ounces) 111
TURNIP GREENS, cooked; ½ cup 9
TURNIPS, cooked without salt, cubed; ½ cup 27
VEAL, cooked
cutlet; 3 ounces 56
loin chop; 3 ounces 55
VEGETABLE JUICE COCKTAIL; 1 cup 535
VINEGAR; 1 tablespoon 0
WAFFLE; 1 section (4½x4½x⅝ inches) 238
WATERMELON; 1 wedge (8x4 inches) 4
YOGURT, plain; ½ cup 63